SECRETS OF
NUMEROLOGY

123456789

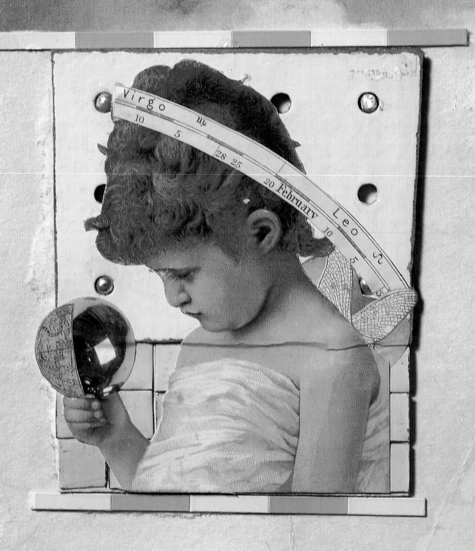

SECRETS OF
NUMEROLOGY

DAWNE KOVAN

IVY PRESS

This edition published in the UK in 2018 by
Ivy Press
An imprint of The Quarto Group
The Old Brewery, 6 Blundell Street
London N7 9BH, United Kingdom
T (0)20 7700 6700 F (0)20 7700 8066
www.QuartoKnows.com

First published in 2001

© 2017 Quarto Publishing plc

British Library Cataloguing-in-Publication Data
A catalogue record for this book is available from the British Library

ISBN: 978-1-78240-573-3

This book was conceived, designed and produced by
Ivy Press
58 West Street, Brighton BN1 2RA, United Kingdom

Art Director: Peter Bridgewater
Editorial Director: Sophie Collins
Design Manager: Anna Stevens
Designers: Kevin Knight, Alistair Plumb, Ginny Zeal
Project Editor: April McCroskie
Picture Researchers: Vanessa Fletcher, Alison Stevens
Photography: Guy Ryecart
Photography organization: Kay MacMullan
Illustrations: Nicky Ackland-Snow, Sarah Young, Andrew Kulman
Three-dimensional models: Mark Jamieson

Printed in China

10 9 8 7 6 5 4 3 2 1

Cover image: Shutterstock/kay mosk

3 4 5 6 7 8 9

Combinations

*The numerical combinations
available to us are infinite.*

HOW TO USE THIS BOOK
This book is designed to take you step by step through the intricacies of numerology. In it, you will find descriptions of the meaning behind the numbers One to Nine and a comprehensive analysis of the Personality Numbers. Methods used for making calculations are carefully explained to enable you to create your own name chart. The section on Prediction lays out straightforward steps to guide you through the labyrinth of techniques available in order to build your confidence in your abilities as a budding numerologist. A case study is provided so that you may examine and compare your findings with it. The final section looks at Numerology's links with astrology and the Tarot.

Important Notice

The final section of the book explores numerology's links with the Tarot. The Tarot is sometimes regarded with suspicion. There is nothing to fear as the cards are simply an ancient method of divination allowing us to understand spiritual patterns and aspirations that run through our lives. However, it is important to foster an attitude of respect for the cards. This will ensure a safe, happy, and rewarding relationship with the Tarot.

Pythagoras
Greek mathematician and mystic, and the father of modern Western numerology.

medicine, and magic had equal stature and were considered one discipline. In later centuries, some aspects of this discipline were rejected by the ruling elite as being mere superstition, which led to its split into separate subjects of study. Numerology and astrology were considered esoteric nonsense, but they still flourished.

Codes, words, & numbers

Ancient peoples instituted codes as a way of preventing sensitive information reaching the unprepared. For example, the Babylonians calculated eclipse cycles and the occurrence of comets but these were regarded with dread and so, in order to protect the populace, this information was encoded. The only people who had access to it were the code-makers themselves.

The Hebrew alphabet served a similar function as both a transmitter of mundane information and a type of coding system. The 22 Hebrew letters were each assigned a number that allowed hidden meanings in certain words to be read only by the initiated, that is, those who had been given the key to the code.

Numerology is also such a code – a code that was taught by the Ancient Greek mathematician Pythagoras in Italy in the sixth century BC. He was an initiate of a number of esoteric schools and later founded his own mystery school to transmit his knowledge to the chosen few.

Much of this work was used subsequently by the Greek philosopher Plato, to develop his own school of thought. His influence continues to reverberate in modern psychology and philosophy, and even in numerology, which contains information that will help people understand themselves and re-establish their link with the spiritual.

Mathematics came to the West from Egypt and the ancient Mesopotamian civilization of Babylonia. The earliest records that we have of an organized mathematical system come from these two cultures and date back to the third millennium BC. In the fourth century BC this system spread to Greece, and so began the mathematics that modern numerology regards as its foundation. Other realities beyond the purely physical were taken seriously by the ancient Egyptians and Babylonians. Thus, mathematics, astronomy, astrology,

Background

*The first section charts the fascinating
development of numerology through the ages.*

Number analysis

Each of numerology's core numbers is explained in detail.

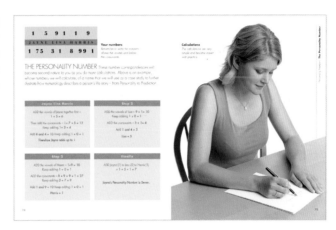

Practical advice

Case studies and easy-to-follow examples help make calculation methods clear.

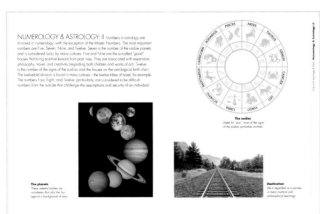

Taking it further

The final section takes a look at numerology's links with astrology and the Tarot.

Introduction

Galileo Galilei

*Astronomer and mathematician
Galileo (1564–1642) recognized
the value of numbers.*

It has been recognized since biblical times that numbers have particular vibrations which have a profound effect on our lives. The early Greeks taught that numbers are central to the understanding of life itself. They claimed that the primary numbers one to nine represent the entire creative process, from the creation of the Universe out of chaos to the rhythms of an individual life. According to scholars of the past, numbers vibrate in tune with the Music of the Spheres – the unique sound made by the planets. In this sense, numerology is linked closely to astrology, which suggests that human life is a reflection and response to cosmic vibrations. Galileo, the medieval Italian astronomer, said, "The book of nature is written in mathematical language." Thus, the language of numbers offers us more than mere verbal communication – it offers us the ability to order and control our lives.

The language of numbers

Once we learn to apply the language of numbers to our lives, the future may not seem so haphazard. By learning the meaning of numbers in all their forms, we can begin to understand more about ourselves, and our potential and motives. Understanding how our Destiny (or Life Path), Personality, and Soul numbers are linked together helps us express who we really are. We begin to recognize the rhythms and patterns within us which make us unique. This will help us to make new choices based on self-knowledge and understanding.

We can use the same tools to find out about the people who accompany us in our lives and gain insight into how and why our relationships may or may not work. We can even apply numerology to cities and nations in order to understand national characteristics or to find the ideal place to take a holiday.

What makes numerology exciting is that it opens the door on many new possibilities. Rather than simply enduring the effects of various life circumstances, we can, through numerology, take part in the rhythmic process that links us with universal purpose and meaning.

Music of the Spheres

The ancient Greeks believed that each planet in the Solar System had a unique sound, resonating with the harmony of the Universe, called the Music of the Spheres.

HISTORY

Numerology is mentioned in sacred literature from all over the world, which suggests that it had great significance for ancient writers. Each culture used a different numerical system. Europe's system can be traced back to Egypt, Babylon, Greece, and Rome. Many mathematical concepts were given to Europeans by the Arabs, whose culture flowered while the West was in the Dark Ages. The ancient cultures that gave birth to the study of mathematics also believed in divination. This indicates that ancient cultures observed a connection between God (or spiritual realms) and humankind that we do not fully understand today. Modern thinking reduces mathematics to an intellectual pursuit and does not appreciate its link with the Divine. Numerology attempts to restore that link.

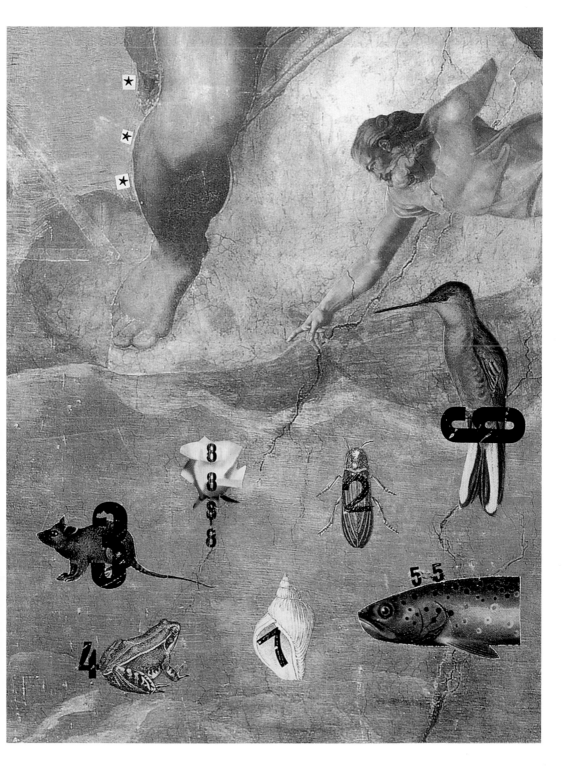

The History of Numerology

Pythagoras
*Greek mathematician and mystic,
and the father of modern Western
numerology.*

Mathematics came to the West from Egypt and the ancient Mesopotamian civilization of Babylonia. The earliest records that we have of an organized mathematical system come from these two cultures and date back to the third millennium BCE. In the fourth century BCE this system spread to Greece, and so began the mathematics that modern numerology regards as its foundation. Other realities beyond the purely physical were taken seriously by the ancient Egyptians and Babylonians. Thus, mathematics, astronomy, astrology, medicine, and magic had equal stature and were considered one discipline. In later centuries, some aspects of this discipline were rejected by the ruling elite as being mere superstition, which led to its split into separate subjects of study. Numerology and astrology were considered esoteric nonsense, but they still flourished.

Codes, words & numbers

Ancient peoples instituted codes as a way of preventing sensitive information reaching the unprepared. For example, the Babylonians calculated eclipse cycles and the occurrence of comets but these were regarded with dread and so, in order to protect the populace, this information was encoded. The only people who had access to it were the code-makers themselves.

The Hebrew alphabet served a similar function as both a transmitter of mundane information and a type of coding system. The 22 Hebrew letters were each assigned a number that allowed hidden meanings in certain words to be read only by the initiated, that is, those who had been given the key to the code.

Numerology is also such a code –
a code that was taught by the Ancient
Greek mathematician Pythagoras in Italy
in the sixth century BCE. He was an initiate
of a number of esoteric schools and
later founded his own mystery school to
transmit his knowledge to the chosen few.

Much of this work was used
subsequently by the Greek philosopher
Plato, to develop his own school of
thought. His influence continues to
reverberate in modern psychology and
philosophy, and even in numerology,
which contains information that will help
people understand themselves and
re-establish their link with the spiritual.

George Washington
*He sought freedom and unity
for his nation, the United States.
These ideals are typical of a
Number Five person such as
Washington.*

CODE Numerology can be understood as a code that contains information about people's lives. The Platonic ideals that are encapsulated in the numbers of this numerological code take a slightly different form in each person who embodies their vibrations. When we consider historical figures, or people in the public eye, we begin to see how numbers are expressed as human experience. Famous people who embody or express their Personality numbers in the purest form possible are just as rare as ordinary people who do. The careers famous people choose often provide hints about what they really wish to express in their lives. But whether famous or just an ordinary person, by uncovering the hidden meanings of the numbers associated with each name chart we are able to gain a better understanding of ourselves and so re-establish the divine connection that has been lost through the years.

J.K. Rowling
*As a Number Four, J.K. Rowling
uses her gifts as a communicator
to reach out and spread her
magical message to her enormous
fan base. Her Harry Potter stories
draw from traditional esoteric
knowledge.*

Mark Zuckerberg

*A true visionary Number Seven,
Mark Zuckerberg spread his social
media technology worldwide, enabling
millions to connect across the globe. The
breadth of his reach is breathtaking.*

Charles Darwin

*As a Five, this biologist attempted
to free humankind from traditional
and out-dated ideas through his
theory of evolution.*

Brigitte Bardot

*The famous beauty and actress
embodies the sensuality of the
number Six. She is also a tireless
worker for animal rights'
organizations.*

Esoteric Teachers

G.I. Gurdjieff

Gurdjieff's system for self-development was known to his students as The Work.

Georgei Ivanovitch Gurdjieff (1877–1949), the Russian mystic and teacher, spent a few years in Tibet as a Buddhist monk. He discovered an ancient nine-pointed star, known as an Enneagram, and brought it to the West, where he used it as a numerological device for teaching people profound truths about themselves. Also said to have been influenced by Tibetan masters, the early twentieth-century British mystic Alice Bailey taught what she termed the Seven Rays. She believed that the Sun, Moon, and five planets emanated energy rays, and that each individual responded to one particular ray. Bailey claimed that what she knew came from her teacher, a Tibetan master.

First taught as part of Theosophy, Bailey's Seven Rays theory was later developed by Roberto Assagioli, the founder of Psychosynthesis. He devised a system of classifying people according to the Ray their personalities were expressing at a given time and the Ray they were travelling along in life. This is a simple imitation of the two basic principles of numerology – that we each have a Life Path Number and a Personality Number that shape our lives.

Ancient & modern

Both Gurdjieff and Alice Bailey brought secret ideas from Tibet to the West. This suggests that numerology was part of ancient Eastern philosophies and mystery schools. Gurdjieff's Enneagram work was so successful that it continues to be used in psychological typology.

Today numerologists work with both private and corporate clients. Many people are interested in who they are and where they are going in life. A numerology reading offers them insights into these questions and helps them to understand their relationship needs.

Corporate clients have much the same questions to ask as an individual. Numerology can reveal new choices and possibilities that they may not have thought of before, thus widening their horizons. It can also assist managers with personnel recruitment by helping them find the right person for a job. The insight into the way people function and interrelate is invaluable to any employer.

The Enneagram

Literally a "picture of nine", the Enneagram is used to describe the nine modalities of human behaviour, which are also revealed through the study of numerology.

UNIVERSAL NUMBERS

The Universal Numbers are the numbers One to Nine, plus the so-called Master Numbers 11 and 22. Zero is also included here because it has an influence on some compound numbers that appear in the days of the month. All compound numbers can be reduced by the addition of their digits to any number between One and Nine. The Universal Numbers are archetypes, and therefore represent the purest expression of each number's qualities. Later we will look at how each Universal Number becomes personalized by calculating the Destiny (or Life Path), Personality, and Soul Numbers of an individual. Everyone has a combination of these three numbers. We must begin, however, with the eleven basic tools of numerology in order to understand how we express the energy vibration idealized by each number.

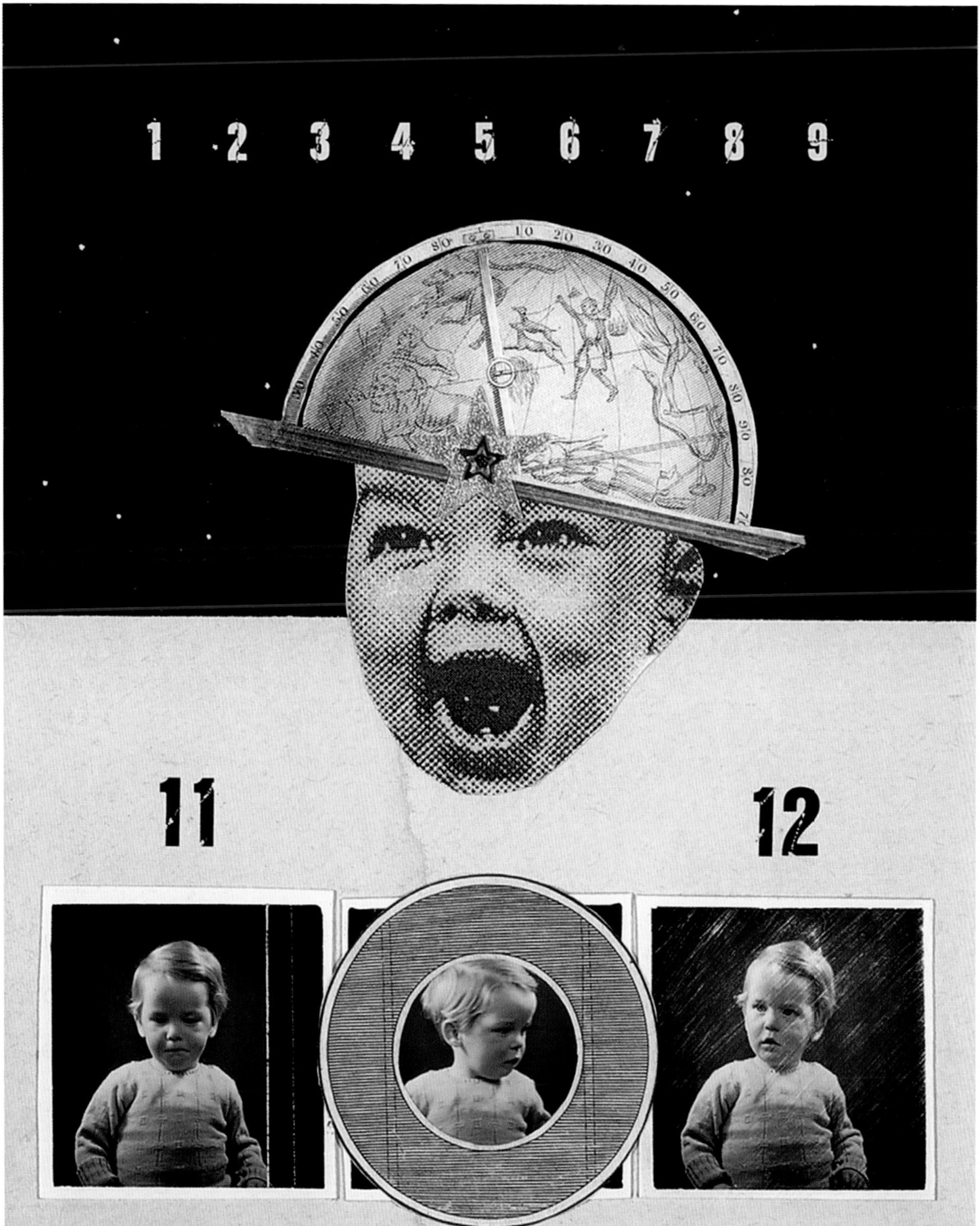
1 2 3 4 5 6 7 8 9
11
12

Theory of Universal Numbers

Dr C.G. Jung

Many of the terms Jung used to describe psychological processes have found their way into our everyday language.

Carl Gustav Jung (1875–1961), the Swiss psychologist, described an archetype as a pure expression of an ideal that is common to all cultures. In this sense, Universal Numbers represent archetypes or ideals that anyone from any belief system or religion may recognize as containing essential truths. The pure qualities of number One, for example, run like a clear stream when it expresses itself in its essential form. No matter how much its expression may be changed by life's experiences, its essence remains constant.

It is important to study the Universal Numbers first, as they contain different qualities that may never be expressed in a single lifetime by one person. Each of us has a combination of these universal principles, which are expressed through the Destiny (Life Path) or Soul Number, for example, but they are not all available to us all of the time.

Through our everyday lives, from childhood, we learn to strengthen one part of ourselves and deny another part, often to our detriment. Through numerology, we can rediscover the parts we have denied by noting where each Universal Number pops up in our numerology chart, and the qualities it demonstrates. But we must first find out what these qualities are.

Seeing yourself in the numbers

Keeping a record of the numbers that are significant in our lives can help us observe how they affect us – even telephone numbers can have an influence on our lives. A number may be strongly emphasized in the chart of someone to whom you were close in childhood, while another may be strong in the chart of a person whom you currently have difficulty getting along with. Remember, these numbers are not who you are, or who they are, but show different ways in which personalities are expressed.

Each Universal Number is illustrated by some well-known people whose lives strongly demonstrate the particular qualities of its vibrations. This shows how different people reflect the same ideals in different – and sometimes surprising – ways. It may also help you to understand that the deeper motivations driving an individual's life may not be easily discerned.

The Sun

Sometimes called the Lord of the Sky, the Sun is the central point around which the other planets revolve.

ONE – THE PIONEER

Number One is the first number in the sequence and represents everything that is new, untried, and fresh. It is the first odd number, and is masculine and outgoing. It is the stage of human development that we all experience at the beginning of our lives when everything we do is challenging, exciting, and heroic. Number One is the Solar Hero figure in mythology – Apollo, the Sun God, who drives his golden chariot across the sky. Each dawn, welcomed by birdsong, the Sun God rises triumphant, banishing the darkness. He measures the day by carrying the Sun across the firmament, until he sets it in the West, journeying through the Underworld to be reborn the following morning.

The name's Bond. . .

James Bond is the archetypal heroic number One – courageous, focused, and powerful. Sean Connery, the first movie Bond, also has a One Life Path.

John Lennon
A creative, pioneering musician, Lennon was also aggressive and energetic – like all Number Ones.

Charlie Chaplin
Portraying his original tramp character, Chaplin exhibited his individuality – a Number One trait

Number One	
PRINCIPLE	Masculine. The positive and active principle. The First Cause out of which all things tumble into life. The Seed. Birth. Initiation. The Alpha. Number One can be divided or multiplied by itself and still retain its individuality. In religions, it is God, the Lord, the One above all others, the Monad, the Godhead, Yahweh.
EGO FUNCTION	Individuality, independence, purpose, strength, originality, choice, and decision.
HIGHEST QUALITY	Individuation, selfhood, and self-assertion.
MODALITY	Action.
ELEMENT	Fire.
RULING PLANET	The Sun.
PEOPLE	Victors, emperors, and kings.
FAMOUS ONES	Charlie Chaplin, the "funniest man in the world"; Margaret Thatcher, first British woman Prime Minister; John Lennon, ex-Beatle; Sean Connery, a convincing James Bond.

Number One

Number One

Ones are movers and shakers who have an effect on everyone around them.

To Ones, the beginning of any project is the most interesting, but they don't stay around to be bored by the everyday running of their inventions. This is fine so long as they have a team to take care of the details for them. And most Ones do, as they make good leaders and company directors. Their successes in life do not come from a desire for money or power, but as the result of their innate self-confidence and ability to focus on their projects.

Ambitious Ones are Alpha types who are courageous, daring, and true pioneers. They need to be at the head of the queue, and are ready to grab the next great challenge and run with it. Ones have very fast reactions and do most of their thinking on their feet.

Fighting spirit, active life

Ones are able to take prompt and decisive action, and have courage and the power to conquer both their surroundings and other people. This can be useful in any competitive situation, but can cause them problems if they are involved in team sports. They are too individualistic to enjoy conforming to a group. They make good coaches for

Number Ones leap into life and approach the world directly. They are the innovators of the world, and need a lot of space in order to express their uniqueness without compromise. They are naive and tend to rush into situations with a childlike faith, never thinking for one moment that the rest of the world may see things differently to them. Their spontaneous freshness is charming and can be irresistible to others.

those less able than themselves and can encourage other people to overcome their fears.

Ones are not sentimental, nor do they dwell on the past. They prefer to burn their bridges behind them and strike out into fresh new adventures. Mentally, they are alert and combative. They enjoy energetic discussions and will sometimes argue for argument's sake. They love to win and are quick and incisive with their words. The saying, "If you can't stand the heat, then get out of the kitchen," must have been invented by a One.

The Individual

The basis of everything is found in One so Number Ones have a tendency to feel extra special. As a result they often show off, or have an individual dress sense.

Yin and Yang
The Chinese symbol for the perfect balance in nature between masculine and feminine characteristics.

TWO – THE PARTNER

Number Two is the point in the sequence where we begin to recognize our difference from others. It is the moment when the individual ego separates from the Mother but still yearns for union with her. The search is then on for the Soulmate, the One, who will become the centre of our lives once more. Two is even and feminine, and yearns for completion through relationships. Number Two is the Heroine in mythology. It is exemplified by Artemis, Lunar Goddess and twin of Apollo, who is a huntress. She is armed with a sickle-shaped bow and protects little children and all suckling animals. Her gift to humankind is the light of the night sky, the Moon. She measures the month with her ever-changing phases and controls the tides.

Adele
Adele is a typical Two who is able to mine her own relationship experiences. She sings about love and loss with great power touching the hearts of millions.

The Moon
Ancient peoples believed the moon symbolized the Goddess and the divine Feminine principle.

Jackie Kennedy Onassis
This famous Two was the wife of two powerful husbands.

Number Two

PRINCIPLE	Feminine, duality, fluctuation. Two signifies receptivity, passivity, the attraction and union of opposites, the mystical marriage, Yang and Yin, the drive for unity through the knowledge of separation, contrast, and reconciliation. The life-giving maternal energy. Imagination, reflection, and intuition.
EGO FUNCTION	Co-operation, relationship, balance, discernment, desire for justice.
HIGHEST QUALITY	Loving wisdom, unconditional love, fruitfulness.
MODALITY	Reaction to surroundings.
ELEMENT	Water.
RULING PLANET	The Moon.
PEOPLE	Team players, partners, spouses.
FAMOUS TWOS	Jacqueline Kennedy Onassis, wife of two powerful men (a US President and a Greek shipping tycoon); Adele, soulful singer.

Number Two

Inner harmony
Two represents balance and inner peace. Yoga is just one of the traditional methods for achieving this.

Number Twos approach the world through their feelings and are compassionate and imaginative. Intellect and intuition unite well for Twos and they can be seen to be both imaginative and inventive. Their principal interest lies in relating to others, and they define themselves through their relationships. Love is at the core of their belief in life.

Twos are sensitive to the needs of others in their community and the world at large. This can make them interested in ecology, the environment, and social issues. Twos make good carers and nurturers of the weak and helpless. They are also peace-lovers and will always try to bring a measure of equanimity to all their dealings with others.

Twos are team players. They have an almost psychic ability to foresee the development of the game before it happens. For them, winning comes second to participating in the group. Their canny gift of foresight also works for them in their careers and financial negotiations. Not afraid of hard work, they apply themselves with determination and maintain a keen eye on the needs of their group or team.

Supportive & sensitive

Many Twos enjoy being the power behind the throne to more powerful bosses. Their tendency to observe life means that they are able to analyse with great skill, and often see things that the busy leader may miss in his rush to the top. Diplomacy is an innate quality within the psyche of Twos. At any level, they can smooth ruffled feathers, whether they are dealing with their squabbling children or the board members of a major company.

The sensitivity of Twos to the feelings and needs of those around them can make them feel that making decisions is tough. Because they find it painful to hurt people's feelings, choosing one person over another to perform some function, or deciding which employee they have to get rid of if their company is having financial difficulties, can be a minefield for them.

Marriage and partnerships are easy for Twos to handle. Their difficulty lies in spending time alone and pursuing solitary paths. This is why meditation is so good for their health. Twos need to find balance and harmony in their lives in order to develop emotional stability and strength.

Balancing Act

Number Twos like to weigh up the pros and cons in life, but have difficulty making decisions – perhaps because they are unwilling to listen to reason.

Fairytales
The number Three crops up in many traditional children's stories.

THREE – THE COMMUNICATOR

Number Three is the result of the marriage between the positive and negative One and Two. It is the number that embodies the creative urge – that which is produced from the tension of the duality. It is a masculine and odd number and, therefore, outgoing. Many fairy stories repeat the theme of Three – the spell that must be repeated three times, a question asked three times, a bell rung three times. Number Three is represented in mythology by the Triple-headed God or Goddess found in many ancient traditions. The powers of creation, continuation, and destruction lie in Three people. They are linked with the seasonal changes that the Earth goes through annually as it orbits the Sun. Three is also the Trinity of the Sun, Moon, and Earth and is symbolized in much religious imagery: for example, by the Egyptian holy family of Osiris, Isis, and Horus.

Ed Sheeran
Ed Sheeran embodies the light and airy nature of Number Three – he began his songwriting career while still in his early teens. He is one of the most downloaded singers of all time.

Confucius

This founder of Chinese philosophy spoke of taking the Middle Path or the Third Way, expressing the Three trait of craving to develop their own ideas.

Chelsea Clinton

Famous first daughter, as a Number Three she worked as a TV journalist. She now heads The Clinton Foundation, set up by her parents.

Number Three

PRINCIPLE	The divine child. The creation out of the union between One and Two, mother and father. The Holy Trinity. Expansion into life. Breadth, optimism, and enthusiasm. Joy. Active intelligence. Utopian, idealistic, hopeful, positive, and sanguine. Abundance. Creativity.
EGO FUNCTION	The drive to communicate, self-expression through the mental processes.
MODALITY	Speaking.
ELEMENT	Air.
RULING PLANET	Jupiter.
PEOPLE	Communicators, lecturers, ministers of the church, dancers, and comedians.
FAMOUS THREES	Confucius, Chinese philosopher; John Travolta, actor; Ed Sheeran, songwriter; Chelsea Clinton, activist.

Number Three

Versatile and alert
*Threes excel when
they are required to unite
mind and body.*

Number Threes approach life through their mental processes. They make good counsellors and advisers, offering a fine blend of good, common-sense wisdom and well-grounded guidance. Their positive and good-humoured attitude to life means that they always tell stories and jokes that expand our understanding of the world around us.

They have wide-ranging interests and find everything fascinating. Threes make gifted teachers, particularly of the very young, as they are able to stimulate the interests and fire the imaginations of their little charges. Threes are the eternal children of the numbers and seem to keep their wonderment about the world and its happenings.

The urge to communicate motivates many Threes to take careers in journalism and various information technologies. They also make good mathematicians and musicians, although they may prefer to write music rather than perform. They think logically and are able to organize their ideas well. Threes are experimenters and enjoy inventing practical solutions to problems. They dislike sitting still for long and like to be on the move, preferably doing something useful.

Huge appetite for life
Number Threes are optimistic, fun-loving, and generous. Tomorrow, they believe, is a brand new day, with brand new opportunities. They are social and friendly. The entertainment industry is full of Threes. They make good dancers, mimics, and actors. Like all the odd numbers, Threes are outgoing and extrovert. Their energy levels are high, making them lively, ebullient, and sometimes, for those around them, exhausting.

Like Ones, Threes are self-motivating and prefer to be in a position of authority rather than servitude. If they have the freedom to do so, they crave developing their own ideas. They often make valuable, if somewhat maverick, employees.

Spiritually, Threes have interesting unconventional beliefs. They take a bite of this and a nibble of that to create their very own highly personalized mystical system. Even if they are working within a traditional religious framework, their gift for oration and inspiration will lift their congregation to stretch their minds and hearts, and to take a leap into the unexplored regions of their traditional teachings.

The Trinity Number

With their great sense of humour Threes can be superficial and frivolous, but they are also interested in subjects such as philosophy, mysticism, and religion.

The Earth
*Our home is symbolic of all that
is stable and eternally reliable.
It is the icon of the New Age.*

FOUR – THE BUILDER
Four sets ideas in stone and consolidates them. It represents boundaries and limitation on the material plane. Without Four, many ideas would vanish in a puff of smoke. Reality as we experience it would not exist. Number Four is the number of density, substance, and deliberation. It is represented by the biblical story of Noah, whom God instructed to build the Ark in order to save the few righteous people and innocent living creatures on the planet from the flood He sent down to wash the world clean of sinners. All those Noah had saved went on to replenish the Earth, restoring it to its former beauty and fruitfulness.

Number Four	
PRINCIPLE	The material world. Reality. The solid. The square and the cube. Structure. Bringing ideas into form. Artistic realization. Political statesmanship. Pragmatism. Stoicism. Organization. Trustworthiness and reliability. Logical thought. The sciences. The four human functions – physical, emotional, mental, and spiritual. The four cardinal points – North, South, East, West.
EGO FUNCTION	Self-restraint and separation from others. Recognition of uniqueness.
MODALITY	Inertia.
ELEMENT	Earth.
RULING PLANET	The Earth.
PEOPLE	Scientists, sculptors, farmers, gardeners, technicians, builders.
FAMOUS FOURS	Julius Caesar, Roman emperor; Bill Gates, founder of Microsoft.

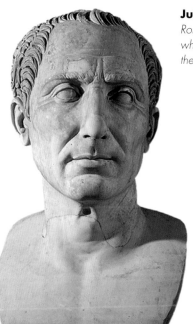

Julius Caesar
Roman Emperor and great general,
who extended and consolidated
the Roman Empire.

The four points of the compass
The four cardinal points give security and
direction to travellers and explorers.

Bill Gates
Like many Fours, this computer genius
and founder of the Microsoft computing
empire brought his ideas into form.

35

Number Four

Traditional family values
Established and conventional social groupings embody Four's stable energy.

Number Fours approach life cautiously and carefully. They like to measure and weigh all their interactions with others. They readily invest in relationships and like to receive a good percentage of interest from their investments. They are financially careful and do not spend their assets unwisely.

Fours have a philosophy based on doubt. They never take anything at face value, preferring instead to test all possibilities before making any kind of judgement. They are not crowd pleasers and prefer to walk alone. Their independence of thought and deed can make them seem isolated, but they are rarely lonely. They prefer their own company to wasting time unproductively with others.

Life moves slowly for Fours. They are the masters and manipulators of time. They are able to plan for the future and execute their schemes at the most opportune moments. "Wait and see" is a favourite expression of Fours, as they watch the unfolding of events dispassionately. They are prepared to play the long game and will climb the ladder patiently, rung by rung, to reach their ultimate goal.

Life in the slow lane

Fours work hard to support those who rely upon them. They do not make commitments lightly, but, once committed, they remain loyal and dedicated. Fours can be idealistic and innovative in social politics, because they want the best for humanity. However, Fours' fixity and inertia can prevent them from recognizing that an idea has passed its sell-by date.

Fours live in the real world and have a strong down-to-earth quality about them. They are sensual and practical, and make decisions based upon how things feel to the touch rather than how they appeal to the mind. Pragmatic and well organized, Fours are high achievers in any occupation that has good, solid foundations.

Responsibility and duty are old-fashioned values that Fours love to live by. They make good lawyers and also do well in the armed forces, and are prepared to lay down their lives to protect their traditions from potential invaders. Parenthood is also very important to Fours, and they take to it wisely and responsibly.

Friendly Fours

Number Fours make good, loyal friends as they are keen to invest a lot of time and energy in maintaining long-term friendships. Fours are also creative and passionate.

Mercury
The planet of intellect and free thinking. Fives are fast talkers and clever wheeler-dealers.

FIVE – THE FREE SPIRIT

Number Five is ruled by Ether, which is beyond the material plane of existence and stimulates life into action. It is linked with the five senses – hearing, touching, seeing, tasting, and smelling – and the five organs in our bodies – the brain, heart, liver, lungs, and kidneys; with the five fingers on each hand, and the five toes on each foot. Number Five is linked to freedom and the search for an ideal way of life. It is exemplified in the biblical story of Moses who, aided by God, freed the Hebrew slaves from captivity in Egypt. The new state that the Hebrews created thereafter was said to have the word of God as its foundation.

Number Five	
PRINCIPLE	Active, inventive, creative, outgoing, seeker of knowledge. Teacher, student. Versatility, curiosity, liveliness, flexibility, sociability, adaptability, change. Love of freedom on all levels of being – physical, emotional, intellectual, and spiritual. The power of information.
EGO FUNCTION	The urge to experience life in its fullness. The need to defend the right of freedom for everyone.
MODALITY	Imagination.
ELEMENT	Ether, the most elusive and extraordinary element.
RULING PLANET	Mercury, the ruler of the marketplace.
PEOPLE	Writers, poets, visionaries, adventurers, inventors, idealists.
FAMOUS FIVES	George Washington, first US President; Charles Darwin, biologist; John Cleese, comedian; Madame Blavatsky, Theosophist; Angelina Jolie, actor.

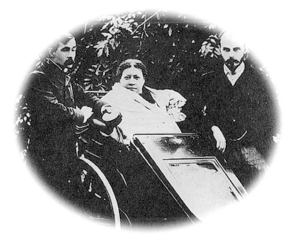

Angelina Jolie

Academy Award-winning actor. She is also a humanitarian, winning awards as an advocate for refugees and for her work in conservation.

Madame Blavatsky

Many Fives are visionaries. Mme Blavatsky was a Five who founded Theosophy, a belief system designed to unite Eastern and Western religious thought.

Freedom through education

Fives continue to learn and explore ideas throughout their adult lives.

Number Five

Love of learning
Fives are interested in everything and will collect a string of diplomas that reflect their hunger for knowledge.

Fives are essentially adventurers, risk-takers and gamblers. Their natural optimism gives them an unerring ability to know when to pitch for the desired aim, which usually pays off. Financially, Fives are in two minds. In one, they are careless and easy-going and, in the other, canny and shrewd with their money. Everything about Fives is contradictory.

Their duality can mean that Fives may follow one career until mid-life then suddenly change direction and retrain for something completely different, and be equally successful in both. This gift means that they are able to communicate at many levels of society while still appearing authentic and genuine to their audience.

Fives are the intellectual racehorses of all the numbers. They think like lightning and can make decisions in a flash. The only problem is that they can make the opposite decision five minutes later. They like to act in the moment and have little patience when waiting for a bus.

Knowledge is power

Fives are on the ball with whatever new idea is the latest currency. They are always in touch with young people and their culture. Five is a good number for youth leaders and trainers, as it gives a natural ability to empathize with new issues as they arise.

Many Fives are teachers and lecturers in higher education. Their favourite subjects are likely to be politics, human rights, freedom of information, and computers. Fives are champions of education for all because they believe that learning is a key that unlocks many doors. They are not very interested in emotional issues and values, but are inspired by ideas and intellectual possibilities. Fives like to keep moving, but it is the short journey and fast-paced city life that hold their attention most of all. They are particularly interested in cultural pursuits found in the city, and in those issues of the day which attract the notice of the masses.

Fives are indelibly printed like a stick of rock candy with the word "freedom" running through them. They will fight for the right of everyone to have freedom of thought and action. If this sounds like the American Constitution, then it is worth pointing out that the United States has a Five birthday. President George Washington was also a number Five.

Brain Power

The essential key to good health for a Five is to keep learning, reading, and talking. With constant stimulation, the "grey matter" will remain optimistic and full of life.

Venus
*Planet of love and
beauty, art and service.*

SIX – THE SERVER

Number Six is the point in the sequence where the individual begins to recognize that the needs of others are as important as his own. Six is a combination of an odd and an even number (2x3). This double vibration of the friendly Three makes Six a very sociable number and therefore an easy number for all the other numbers to relate to. The myth that best illustrates the energy of Six is the story of the Sixth Labour of Heracles in which he had to purge the Augean stables. These were huge sheds in which King Augeas kept his prize herd of cattle, and they had not been cleaned for many years. The dung was said to be the cause of disease and plague amongst the land, so cleaning these sheds was vital. Heracles diverted the course of a nearby river and flooded the cowsheds. This sanitized the entire area and restored peace and health to the land.

The Star of David
*One triangle points towards heaven and the other
points towards earth, symbolizing the unity of the
highest and the most fundamental ideals.*

The artist
*The painter embodies the number
Six by using artistic skills to express
perceptions of reality.*

David Attenborough

David Attenborough's television broadcasts promote the care of wildlife worldwide. He serves Planet Earth in typical Six style through spreading awareness of the environment and the challenges to its survival.

The dancer

Many Sixes use their bodies as a tool, honed to the height of fitness and beauty.

Number Six	
PRINCIPLE	The number of days in the Creation. The six-pointed star, representing the union of humanity and God. Creativity. Art. Rhythms of life.
EGO FUNCTION	The development of selflessness.
MODALITY	Sensual and erotic, diplomatic.
ELEMENT	Earth.
RULING PLANET	Venus, the planet of beauty, love, peace, art, and service.
PEOPLE	Artists, lawyers, diplomats, healers.
FAMOUS SIXES	Brigitte Bardot, actress; David Attenborough, broadcaster.

Number Six

Art
Number Six expresses itself through art and beauty, colour, and harmony.

Sixes need to serve others in some capacity. They may work one-to-one with individuals or with the idea of serving the whole of humanity. Generally idealistic, warm, and compassionate, everything that Sixes do comes from their sense of social responsibility and desire to create a perfect world. Their desire for perfection comes from an awareness of imperfection in themselves and others. Health is a subject very dear to their hearts. They recognize that, in order to do their best, they must have a body that serves them. Sixes are interested in diet and fitness programmes which aim to create the perfect body. Their interest in their own well-being extends to their environment and their friends and neighbours.

Many Sixes are found working at an organizational level for local and world peace, harmony, and justice. They dedicate their lives to struggling against the tides of injustice, and are champions of underdogs. The element of Earth in their make-up gives Sixes an innate practicality and strong sense of responsibility.

Beauty & harmony

Sixes are keenly sensitive to form and beauty which they can see all around them. Since art is the practical expression of a sharp aesthetic sense, they have a strong drive to create beautiful works, which comes in part from this sense, but also from a desire to have a hand in the creative process. Many painters, illustrators, and architects are Sixes, as are art critics and art historians. Many Sixes are multi-skilled and can paint, draw, sculpt, and write with equal ability and giftedness. Even if they do not create great works of art, Sixes will decorate their homes, offices, or gardens with beautifully balanced colours and a peaceful, harmonious ambience. They need to be totally immersed in beauty.

Sixes create beautiful relationships. They strive for harmony and wish to see a peaceful outcome in all disputes. Relating is important to Sixes – they need another person as a counterbalance to themselves. However, not wishing to immerse themselves in another person, they relate as an equal to their partner. Their refined tastes and gentle manner make them attractive to others and they are rarely alone in life.

Give & Take

Their innate fair-mindedness means that Sixes are happy to give and take plenty of free rein in their relationships. Sixes also work long and hard to serve their ideals.

Spirituality
*The candle flame reflects the
state of the inner soul.*

SEVEN – THE DREAMER
Number Seven is the mystical number of all religions. It represents the point in human development where the individual is beginning to have insight into a larger or greater order of existence than the purely personal. These glimpses of a divine reality offer someone the possibility of interpreting experiences in a new light and developing a philosophy to explain them. The Bible story that best reflects the number Seven tells of Daniel's dream that the Pharaoh would have seven fat years followed by seven lean years.

Number Seven	
PRINCIPLE	The Seven visible planets. The Seven days of the week. The Seventh day of rest taken by God in the story of Creation. The Seven colours of the rainbow. The Seven branches of the menorah, the sacred Hebrew candelabrum. The Seven chakras, or energy points, of the human body.
EGO FUNCTION	Interpretation of reality to find meaning in life. The mediation between the individual ego and the divine.
MODALITY	Active and abstract.
ELEMENT	Air.
RULING PLANET	Neptune.
PEOPLE	Philosophers, scientists, educators, writers.
FAMOUS SEVENS	Nostradamus, astrologer and seer; Isaac Newton, visionary scientist; Diana, Princess of Wales.

The stargazer
The astronomer sees a reality far beyond the vision of ordinary humankind.

Another reality
Like looking for gold at the end of the rainbow, Seven's true goal lies beyond the physical world.

Isaac Newton
This eminent scientist and mathematician was a Seven who devoted much of his time to the study of theology. Sevens frequently search for the essential meaning of life.

Number Seven

The philosopher
*Seven offers his most profound thoughts
to the world.*

Number Sevens are deep thinkers and have profound insights into the nature of humanity. They are idealistic and natural philosophers. Sevens are kind-hearted and romantic. They view life through rose-coloured spectacles and are sympathetic, sentimental, and sometimes noble. The sympathies of Sevens are turned towards the suffering of humans and animals, and many are social workers, animal rights' activists, and vegetarians. They desire justice and happiness for all and want everyone to live in an ideal world. Sevens are not party animals. They prefer their own company and are naturally introspective.

Self-sufficient and independent, they are rarely lonely. Their solitary nature belies a deeply sensitive and emotional side. Many Sevens are highly sensitive to others and can be gifted with psychic abilities.

Idealistic and visionary, Sevens loathe social injustice. Their weapon is the pen – or word processor – with which they write many learned papers, essays, and letters in the hope that they can make a difference. Sevens are very creative in their use of words and often produce strikingly imaginative poetry and prose. They spin complex images and weave fascinating fairytales.

New spirituality for a New Age

The spirituality of Sevens is attuned to that of the New Age. They are mystics and metaphysicians.

Sevens make natural healers, and prefer the holistic approach to medicine and health. They can be highly technical and intuitive scientists. Meditation, fasting, and spiritual practices are the stuff of life for Sevens. They love their candles, angel cards, and incense. Their God is universal rather than personal, and they feel that everyone should have the right to worship in their own way. They seek mystical, emotional experiences that will nourish them. Their poetry and drawings often depict the visionary times in which we are living.

The rather abstract approach to life that Sevens often have tends to mean that they are not concerned with material things. This can make them seem like the Cosmic Cowboy, who hangs his hat in many different places. Seven is associated with long-distance travel and wonderment in the mysteries of the Universe. This number gives one the desire to transcend ordinary life.

Virtue & Sin

The morality tales of the Seven Virtues and Seven Deadly Sins were associated with the positive and negative attributes of the Seven astrological planets.

Elizabeth Taylor

This successful actress and focused fund-raiser for AIDS charities was an Eight. Eights often bring people together to attain a group goal.

EIGHT – THE FINANCIER
Eight is the number of power, the power to make things happen and of successful attunement to higher powers. It is also the number of organization and ritual, and of the recognition that without structure and rhythm, energy cannot be organized. It exemplifies the will to make ideas manifest reality. Associated with Eight is the story of King Midas, who prayed to the gods to make him rich. The gods gave him the power to turn everything he touched into gold. As his favourite daughter embraced him, she too turned to gold so he begged the Gods to take back their gift and make her human again.

Number Eight	
PRINCIPLE	Eight is the number of the cube. The three-dimensional material world with the added fourth dimension of time. The symbol for eternity. The double helix of the DNA code.
EGO FUNCTION	The ability to organize the will and power.
MODALITY	Stoicism and dominance.
ELEMENT	Water.
RULING PLANET	Saturn, planet of time and karma.
PEOPLE	Chief executive officers of large corporations, financiers, materialists, judges.
FAMOUS EIGHTS	Elizabeth Taylor, actress and fund-raiser; Barbra Streisand, actress, singer, film director.

Liquid
Eight has the ruling element of Water.

The double helix
Since ancient times this figure-of-eight shape has been a symbol for the power of healing. Today we know it is the shape of the molecular structure of DNA.

Judgement
Eights make good judges as they tend to have strong personalities and have the power to make things happen.

Number Eight

The lawgiver

Eight embodies the ability to make strong decisions and stick to them.

Eights are introverted, reserved, patient, serious, and self-confident. Success, ambition, authority, and leadership go hand-in-hand for them. They are conservative in their attitudes, preferring tradition and well-tried-and-tested methods to cutting-edge innovation. They consider all their options for a long time before making final decisions.

Eights have the ability to turn their own and others' ideas into reality and to make a huge profit for all concerned. Their strong sense of responsibility ensures that they regard their undertakings as sacrosanct.

Eights are loyal and do not break promises. Their sense of honour is strong, binding, and life-long.

Eights are willing to struggle against all the odds to achieve their goals and are prepared to put in many hours and days above the call of duty to ensure the success of a project.

Many Eights start at the bottom of the company where they are working, performing mundane tasks, yet find the climb to the top of the corporate ladder a straightforward, if lengthy, matter. In the area of education Eights are usually heads of department or even of the entire establishment.

Personal power – public life

Eights are interested in humanity, believing that society's ills stem from a lack of financial stability. The financial centres of the world are populated by Eights. The kinds of gifts that Eights have ensure that quite often they are found working in the public arena – usually somewhere in politics, mass media, and communications.

Eights derive great security and certainty from the rites, rituals, and dogma of traditional belief systems. The higher echelons of various religious establishments are the natural domicile of Eights. They make good heads of their orders.

Eights are empirical thinkers and only trust information that they can personally verify. They rarely take chances and are cautious in all undertakings. In both games and life, simply taking part is not enough for Eights – they must win. Good at wars of attrition, they are best at using their strong wills to bring people together for some kind of co-operative effort, particularly when working towards a group goal or aim.

King Canute

He believed himself to be more powerful than the ocean's tides. In dismay, he watched as the sea refused to stop at his command and threatened to drown him and his courtiers.

9

Container
This number contains all the other numbers.

NINE – THE PEACEMAKER
Number Nine marks the end of a cycle of progress. The circle is about to become a spiral and start again at number One. Nine is an energetic and restless number, aware of coming changes. It is the drive to achieve for others, to use the will for the good of all and to fight without caring for the outcome. Win or lose, it's all the same to Nine; it is the taking part that matters. The myth that best describes the energy of Nine is the story of Chiron, the Centaur, who was a teacher of young gods and heroes. He taught music, the arts of war, healing, and astrology. When he was wounded accidentally by his pupil, Heracles, he was unable to die, being immortal. He offered to exchange himself for Prometheus, a mortal whom the gods were punishing. As a result Prometheus was allowed to return to live on Earth and Chiron was placed in the sky as the Centaur constellation.

Judy Garland
Nines, like Judy Garland, make good performers, particularly in films.

Flame
Number Nine has the ruling element of Fire.

Che Guevara
This revolutionary embodied the Nine passion for ideals.

Number Nine

PRINCIPLE	Nine is the number that contains all the other numbers. When added to any number other than Nine, it loses itself to that number. (Try it). It is the number of completion and endings. The final turn of the Wheel of Fortune before it starts a new cycle. The Nine months of pregnancy. The Nine muses. The highest single number, therefore the most refined and developed.
EGO FUNCTION	Self-effacement, self-denial, selflessness.
MODALITY	Action.
ELEMENT	Fire.
RULING PLANET	Mars, the Warrior.
PEOPLE	Reformers, humanitarians, freedom-fighters, idealists, surgeons, psychiatrists.
FAMOUS NINES	Judy Garland, singer, entertainer; Richard Branson, entrepreneur; Che Guevara, revolutionary.

Number Nine

The warrior
He is prepared to lay down his life for his ideals.

Nines are selfless towards humanity. Generous with their time, energy, and resources, they often work in charitable and philanthropic organizations. Their innate ability to put their egos aside means that Nines make good actors, particularly in movies. Each time they adopt a new role, they do so with the knowledge that it is teaching them a new lesson about life. Nines are willing to embrace this experience. Well-balanced and integrated, Nines are easy-going and broad-minded. Their humour is never cruel or petty. They love to poke fun at the pompous behaviour of public figures and are clever at satire. However, they never hold a grudge if someone pokes fun back at them. Their attitudes are liberal and they are always willing to forgive and forget.

Nines can be restless and impatient with those who display brutality and are mean-spirited. They are prepared to fight for the rights of others, but do so with great care and strategy. They are the generals of the Universe. Nines prefer to use intelligence rather than physical strength to win their battles, and are skilful in their use of force.

Enthusiasm for change

Nines are practical and realistic in bringing their ideals into reality. They will work long and hard to bring a new state or government into being. Nines will tear down old structures to prepare for the birth of the new, but will not hang around to implement anything after it is set up. Their sights will already be on the next great idea.

Freedom from the senses and the bondage of human desires seems to come

Universal Numbers **Number Nine**

naturally to Nines. They do not involve themselves with the minutiae of human life, preferring the lofty, more rarefied, atmosphere of concepts and absolutes. Showing great patience towards others, Nines make good teachers, especially of practical subjects that develop skills, such as engineering.

Aware that nothing remains the same, Nines have a unique ability to be prepared for whatever life throws their way. They enthusiastically and creatively embrace diversity, and hold to the idea that nothing is forever and that resisting change can be both counterproductive and unhealthy.

Maternity

The pregnant woman carries within her the growing seed of a new generation. She puts her own needs to one side in favour of the needs of her child.

Madonna
This megastar Eleven created powerful new images for young women worldwide to emulate.

ELEVEN – THE VISIONARY

Eleven can mistakenly be reduced to Two, so this must be avoided. It is an odd number that reduces to an even number, which means that someone may appear passive, attractive, and introverted, like other even numbers, but underlying this is the extroverted energy of the odd number that needs to be expressed creatively and originally. Eleven is the number of magic and mystery, and can indicate a strongly developed sixth sense. This comes from the magical union of two totally opposite elements – enigmatic Water and cerebral Air. Eleven has its roots in universal consciousness and brings illumination. The stories of Merlin, the magician who served King Arthur in the legends of Britain, resonate with the characteristics of the number Eleven. Merlin was wise and gifted with clairvoyance. He helped Arthur to become king and to keep control over his lands. Merlin envisioned that the land would be united and that peace would prevail.

The dream team
Many team sports, such as football, have eleven players.

Paul Simon

His thoughtful and haunting songs describe common, rather than personal, themes – in keeping with the concerns of most Elevens.

Prince William

Initially a heroic helicopter rescue pilot, he is now taking on more royal duties along his path to eventually becoming King.

Number Eleven

PRINCIPLE	Eleven is the first compound number to be used in numerology. Known as a Master Number. Only used in exceptional circumstances. Intuition. Foresight. Prophecy. Psychic. Truth. Beauty. Balance of positive and negative. Universal justice. The eleven members of a games team.
EGO FUNCTION	Insight into higher states of consciousness.
MODALITY	Reflective about the meaning of life.
ELEMENT	Mixture of Water and Air.
RULING PLANET	Uranus, the Illuminator.
PEOPLE	Counsellors, teachers of wisdom, psychics, astrologers.
FAMOUS ELEVENS	James Goldsmith, business magnate and ecologist; Paul Simon, singer-songwriter; Madonna, singer, actress; Prince William, heir to the throne.

Number Eleven

Balance
Elevens seek harmony by experiencing disharmonious circumstances.

Many Elevens are found working as therapists or teachers. Personally, they face many challenges, particularly emotionally. These make them ideal for helping others in crisis. Sometimes Elevens stimulate others into making choices, and act as catalysts that can shift attitudes or viewpoints from ignorance to awareness.

Elevens seek meaningful relationships and are altruistic towards their partners. Their innate ability to see the potential within each individual means they encourage its development wherever they perceive it. Elevens are always advised to keep this type of activity reserved for their professional life, so that their partners have the opportunity to make their own decisions.

The painter, writer, or film-maker who has Eleven in his life is able to create images that convey a deeper layer of meaning than usual. These images may not contain mystical subject matter but the message is there all the same. Creative Elevens are truly inspired and their artwork lives on long after they have departed this life, enthralling and giving joy to those who come after them.

Positive & negative

As the higher octave of Two, Eleven is also searching for balance, this time between the ordinary and the extraordinary. Elevens are very tense and their nervous system is highly refined. This gives them increased sensitivity to psychic levels beyond the physical world. They are often highly intuitive and receptive, and make good natural healers. Some Elevens are able to channel thought forms and communicate them in an accessible way.

Elevens are able to soar above the rest of humanity and intuit the meaning of even the simplest human activities. They understand the meaning of life itself by seeing events in their entirety at the abstract level of perception. Many Elevens are guided by their higher selves to follow a professional path of social service or healing.

The key word for Eleven is illumination. They willingly share the light that shines within them with everyone. This is why so many Elevens are at the cutting edge of psychological and spiritual thinking. They possess a rare combination of detachment and interest, which gives them a unique ability to advise and teach others.

Illumination

Eleven is the number of the Light Bringer, who brightens the darkness so that others may see the way safely through ignorance and prejudice.

Eckhart Tolle

His book The Power of Now *earned him the title of "most popular spiritual author in the United States" by the* New York Times. *He is a Life Path Number Twenty-two, bringing together many streams of mystical thought into his writing.*

TWENTY-TWO – THE ARCHITECT
The Master Numbers are rare and are found in exceptional people. Twenty-two is double the energy of Eleven, so gives someone an extremely powerful drive, for good or ill. Creative Fire and the dense power of Earth combine to manifest great cathedrals and pyramids, mirroring the images of the constellations on Earth. Best illustrated by the Creation myths about the origins of the world, Twenty-two illustrates how the deities conceived the Earth and the Heavens.

Oprah Winfrey

Like many Twenty-twos, this broadcaster is a purveyor of tolerance and inner growth.

Number Twenty-two

PRINCIPLE	Twenty-two is the second Master Number. It must never be reduced to a Four when it appears in a reading. Traditionally called "The Master Builder". The 22 letters of the Hebrew alphabet.
EGO FUNCTION	Abstract thought brought into the concrete mind with altruism. Higher self focused through the creative mind.
MODALITY	Deliberation and consideration.
ELEMENT	Fire and Earth.
RULING PLANET	Pluto, the Transformer.
PEOPLE	Architects, builders of large humanitarian organizations, deans of universities.
FAMOUS TWENTY-TWOS	Christopher Reeve, actor; James Lovelock, author of Gaia and eco-system biologist; Oprah Winfrey, television broadcaster; Eckhart Tolle, author.

Pyramid of Khafre
The pyramids are an eternal reminder of the genius of ancient Egyptian architects.

Number Twenty-two

Fire
The element associated with creativity and intuition – the higher human functions.

Twenty-twos are in touch with the level of vibration that is the most difficult to express. However, many Twenty-twos seem to spend large periods of their lives acting through the Four vibration, working at a fairly mundane level. Later, in middle-life, they may become more sensitive to this Master Number's energy and begin to respond to it.

Twenty-twos are gifted at drawing threads together to describe reality and how the wheels of the Universe function. This can make them seem eccentric and idiosyncratic, as others can find it hard to understand them. Many of their ideas are so far ahead of others and on the leading edge of philosophical and social ideologies that they do not yet have words for them.

Twenty-twos are revolutionaries, not in a warrior-like way, but in a gentle, humane way. Rather than striking others over the head with their ideas they encourage them to open their minds. Twenty-twos are intense and enthusiastic about their designs for the future. They are egalitarian and see beyond gender and race. In fact, they dismantle any type of caste system they encounter.

Master builder – head of state

Twenty-twos work with the decision-making processes in life. They can handle and manipulate large sums of money, while looking to channel it into public welfare and education. In the money markets, Twenty-twos can use their finely tuned antennae to make a killing on futures options. Their ideals are at the root of the Age of Aquarius – those of enlightenment and the "common man" – and they are willing to dedicate their lives to achieving them.

Twenty-twos are architects who can incorporate both a cosmic vision and practical solutions in their designs of new social systems or corporations. They are statesmen who are able to tune into the future needs of humanity today, before the needs arise.

Twenty-twos are always on the alert for ways in which the status quo can be challenged and expanded. The newest ideas, in which the boundaries between physics, psychology, and ecology are becoming more blurred and less easily defined, encapsulate the level at which Twenty-twos function and use their creativity. It is important to remember that both Master Numbers are found very rarely.

The Pyramids

These magnificent monuments were designed by ancient Egyptian architects to mirror Heaven on Earth, and to remind people of their place in the Universal scheme of things.

The circle
Symbol of health and integration.

ZERO – THE CIPHER
Zero is not a number in the strict sense. It is not used in numerology because all compound numbers are reduced to a single digit below Nine. Zero is said to contain all the numbers in potential. It is not a number that has a personality type, a destiny to follow, or a soul urge. It is all of these and none of them. It is the Alpha and the Omega, the beginning and the end, the all and everything. The name of God is said to be represented by Zero because it is too powerful to be limited by any other number. Everything that God creates is contained in the pure, undifferentiated form of the circle. The circle of the Zero is symbolic of the spirit. Two Zeros placed side by side create the sign of infinity. The circle is also a symbol for wholeness and health. Everything contained within its rim is safe, while everything outside remains in chaos.

Nature
The Earth, as a complete system that nourishes and sustains itself, reflects Zero's cyclic nature.

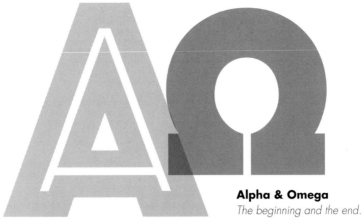

Alpha & Omega
The beginning and the end.

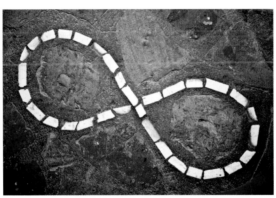

Lemniscate
Ancient symbol of Eternity.

Zero	
PRINCIPLE	Zero is a container, bowl, or crucible. It is pregnant with energy that has not yet taken shape. It adds the power of the unknown to any number to which it is attached.
EGO FUNCTION	It represents the qualities that enable the ego to expand into the unknown.
MODALITY	Zero is still and eternal.
ELEMENT	The primordial soup out of which all life is born.
PEOPLE	There are no social correspondences to Zero.

67

Zero

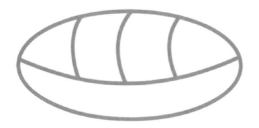

Ancient mathematicians
*The Mayas recognized
the importance of zero in
their mathematics.*

The circle is one of the most basic shapes and it represents zero. Zero has an interesting history that goes back to the beginning of the first century CE. The Babylonians, from whom many of our numerological and astrological teachings come, used written symbols for numbers thousands of years before they invented a symbol for zero. The Hindus were the first to use it and the Hindi word for zero means empty or void.

Later the Arabs introduced Zero to Europe. They used it as a separator between numbers – to differentiate between 11, 101, and 1001, for example. This meant that all numbers could be expressed in terms of ten symbols – the numerals one to nine,

with the addition of zero to make 10. The Mayas of Central America used a symbol for zero in their mathematical annotations in about the first century CE.

In modern technology, zero is used in the binary system in which computer programmes are written. This language is expressed in ones and zeros and can be represented by the positions of on/off switches.

Zero & compound numbers

The simple numbers One to Nine form the basis of numerology, with the addition of the Master Numbers. There is a magical quality to this extraordinary circle digit called zero, because of its connection with spirit and wholeness. It lends a potential for creativity that is formed by the accompanying number. For example, 30 is qualitatively different from 10 or 20 because of the specific attributes of the number 3. The zero, added to the numbers 1, 2, and 3, is found regularly in the digits for the 10th, 20th, and 30th days of each month. The addition of the zero to these single digits adds a particular flavour to their inherent symbolism. For more information on the numbers associated with days of the month, see pages 122–5.

An individual with a zero in any of the basic numbers, either in their name or in their birth date, will have access to energy levels that the simple numbers do not have. Because of the addition of the zero to their numbers, they will find that their gifts are readily available to them and are clearly visible to others. They are linked with the full Moon, another disk or circle, which symbolizes intuition, sensitivity, and psychic abilities.

Full Moon

Eastern astrologers believe that the full Moon indicates a highly auspicious time to be born, endowing a person with public visibility and guaranteeing success in life.

PERSONALITY NUMBERS

The sound of your name when spoken by others connects you with the deepest part of your self and identity. Your Personality Number comes from your name and shows how you express the vibrations of the Universal Number in your own unique way. Your Personality Number contains information about your psychology, relationships, and attitudes towards life. It is made up of many combinations of numbers that are known collectively as your core numbers. Many people ask, "Which name should I use?" The name on your birth certificate vibrates with your soul's reasons for being on earth. While it is true that your birth name is the best starting place, you can also look at your married name or your stage name, if you have one. But you will need to remember that such names are always secondary to your original name.

How to Find Your Personality Number

Here is the way to calculate your Personality Number. Remember, you do not need to be good at maths to do this. Numerology uses no complex techniques. All you have to do is add all the numbers together continually until you arrive at a single digit.

You will need:

- All your birth names written in block capitals.
- The Numerical Values Table (below).

Soon you will learn the values of all these letters by heart and will not need to refer to the table.

Find the values for each letter of your whole name. IMPORTANT "Y" can act as either a vowel or a consonant, depending on its position in a name. If it follows a consonant at the end of a name such as Billy or Mary, then it is calculated as a vowel. If it is part of a compound sound such as "oy" or "ay" as in Roy or Mayfield, then it is calculated as a consonant. In a name such as Boyletty, for example, the first Y is a consonant and the second Y is a vowel. Remember, all letters, whether silent or spoken, are calculated.

The numbers are always written above the vowels and below the consonants

Numerical Values Table								
1	2	3	4	5	6	7	8	9
A	B	C	D	E	F	G	H	I
J	K	L	M	N	O	P	Q	R
S	T	U	V	W	X	Y	Z	

in the name. This makes it easy to
calculate your Karmic Number later on.
As you list the numbers, note which ones
are prominent, either by their absence or
because they are plentiful. These reveal
underlying patterns in the personality that
may not be immediately obvious. Sometimes
these hidden depths can be surprising
and illuminating and sometimes they
can be rather a shock. For example,
an outgoing, pioneering, aggressive
Number One personality may find it
difficult to recognize a conservative
Four lurking somewhere in their profile.

Numbers & Letters

You are now embarking on a fascinating and
revealing study of yourself and those close
to you.

1	5	9 1	1	9

J A Y N E   L I S A   H A R R I S

1	75	3 1	8	99	1

THE PERSONALITY NUMBER These number correspondences will

become second nature to you as you do more calculations. Above is an example, whose numbers we will calculate, of a name that we will use as a case study to further illustrate how numerology describes a person's life story – from Personality to Prediction.

Jayne Lisa Harris

ADD the vowels of Jayne together first –
1 + 5 = 6

Then add the consonants – 1+ 7 + 5 = 13
Keep adding 1+ 3 = 4

Add **6 and 4 = 10** Keep adding 1 + 0 = 1

Therefore Jayne adds up to 1

Step 2

ADD the vowels of Lisa – 9 + 1= 10
Keep adding 1 + 0 = 1

ADD the consonants – 3 + 1= 4

Add 1 and 4 = 5

Lisa = 5

Step 3

ADD the vowels of Harris – 1+9 = 10
Keep adding 1 + 0 = 1

ADD the consonants – 8 + 9 + 9 + 1 = 27
Keep adding 2 + 7 = 9

Add 1 and 9 = 10 Keep adding 1 + 0 = 1

Harris = 1

Finally

ADD Jayne (1) to Lisa (5) to Harris (1)
= 1 + 5 + 1 = 7

Jayne's Personality Number is Seven.

Calculations

The calculations are very simple and become easier with practice.

Calculating the Personality Number

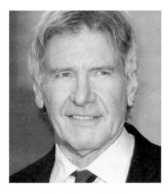

Harrison Ford
Ford is one of the world's most successful actors.

Below is an analysis of the famous actor Harrison Ford's Personality Number. Add all the numbers of his name together like this: Harrison = 1 + 9 + 6 (vowels) + 8 + 9 + 9 + 1 + 5

(consonants) = 48. Then add 4 + 8 =12 = 3. Therefore Harrison has a numerical value of 3.

Follow the same process with the rest of the name and you will find that Ford reduces to 7. The total for the complete name is 3 + 7 = 10 = 1. Therefore, Harrison Ford is a Personality Number One – the number of the Hero and the Pioneer.

Ford's first major role was as Han Solo, the maverick pilot, in George Lucas's astonishingly successful movie Star Wars. The calculation for the Personality Number of Han Solo reduces to number 3 – the number of exploration and expansion, clearly reflecting the personality of the character. The success of the role was

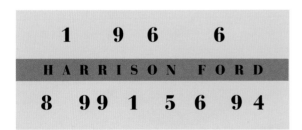

First steps
The name and its numerical equivalents are written like this.

helpfully underpinned by Ford's heroic Number One Personality.

This indicates one of the mysteries of numerology – how a name can reveal so much about who and what we are. Successful people always have a clear match between their numbers and their roles in life. This implies that by knowing your numbers you can ensure that you make the most of your potential, as Harrison Ford is doing.

His pioneering spirit, a trait of One personalities, also led Ford to be the first actor to insist that in addition to his salary for acting, he should also receive a share of the box-office takings of all his films. This has made him a multi-millionaire and a household name.

Han Solo

The name Solo implies a Number One personality and lends extra weight to the fact that the role was perfect for Ford.

Perfect partners
Ones and Twos always find each other.

PERSONALITY ONE & TWO: I One and Two, the first two numbers,
also act as a pair, complementing and defining each other. What One is, Two is not. They are polar opposites, without which the whole could not function. They represent Father and Mother, and all the numbers that follow them are created out of their union. One and Two seek each other in order to find completion, and also tend to create myths and ten-act operas about this eternal search.

Personality Number One
One is an odd and extroverted number which produces an active, innovative personality that others recognize as stimulating. The One personality is vital and visibly filled with self-confidence. The One seeks new horizons and gains strength from each new courageous pursuit. One is the hunter, provider, and protector of the clan. Personality One is like the knight of old who lived by an ancient code of honour and rose to every challenge with enthusiasm.

The preservers

Twos often collect traditional artworks from different cultures.

Collectors

Two personalities are gatherers and often collect items, such as stamps or model cars, as a hobby.

Personality Number Two

Two is even and introverted. It produces an emotional and reflective personality. The Two personality searches for balance and harmony through relationships with others, either in a one-to-one situation or through belonging to a team or group. A Two personality makes a good partner and supporter which the more active numbers may bounce off from. Two is cool and strong and can resist challenges by ignoring them. Two is a gatherer, a collector, and a preserver of tribal traditions.

Personality One & Two: II

Ready for anything
Ones like to be prepared for
whatever life throws at them.

For Ones, being first is close to a religion. They push through all blockages head first and rush into every new situation in order to stand in front of others. Subtle they are not.

In childhood, Ones are happiest as the eldest of the family or as the only child since they can feel hostile and frustrated with older siblings unless they are allowed to develop and shine.

In relationships, Ones follow their desires and are always falling in and out of lust. They demand a great deal of space from their, often long-suffering, partners – not necessarily to have a new liaison, but simply to play at playing the field. They are passionate lovers, so long as their interest is held by their loved ones, and are fun to be with. But Ones continually move the goalposts, which their partners find either stimulating or exhausting, depending on their make-up.

On the negative side, Ones can confuse aggression with self-assertion and sometimes go over the top when trying to make a point. They can be selfish. Some Ones are too dependent, needy, and angry because they lack confidence to express their real One natures.

What turns Personality Two on?
Two personalities need time to trust and reflect. Often their feelings are so deeply hidden they do not know what they are. Still, they use them to judge and respond to life. Their gift is that they understand the importance of their emotional life and therefore make good counsellors and therapists. Their sensitivity to the pain of others can be their strong point in a crisis.

Twos actively seek company and companionship to avoid being alone and may put up with a relationship that has long since passed its sell-by date rather than strike out on their own. They are good partners and are willing to give support and care to all those they love. The changeability of Twos can make them seem mysterious and alluring to their lovers.

The negative aspect of this influence means that Twos will avoid taking risks and opt instead for safety. They can be reclusive and will steer clear of relationships if they cannot control their over-sensitivity.

Often Two personalities shift and change like the tides of the ocean and can be extremely indecisive. They also put themselves second and never take the initiative, much to the frustration of their partners.

Gifted Twos

Their innate ability to reflect the feelings of others makes Twos ideally placed to be counsellors or therapists.

Playpens
Threes hate them, Fours love them.

PERSONALITY THREE & FOUR: | Three and Four, the next pair of numbers in the sequence, both arise out of form. Number Three is the sum of One and Two; it is the created object – the Child. Number Four is the playpen that contains the wild impulses of Three to protect it from harm and keep its toys – its ideas – from being lost. Together Three and Four represent the mental stimulation that drives the urge to communicate and the structure and grammar of language.

Wanderlust
Three's favourite song could well be Don't Fence Me In.

Personality Number Three
Three is the desire to communicate with others through the use of the mental processes. It is an odd and extrovert number, like One, and seeks to express itself actively. The Three personality flows expansively outwards into the world and embraces everything it meets. Three personalities are talkers and walkers and cover a great deal of ground, both physically and mentally. More than any other Personality Number, Three is intrinsically good at heart and forgiving of the mistakes of other people. This optimism attracts others, who bring new information and stimulate new ideas.

Communicating Threes
The bigger the audience the happier Threes are in life.

Weight training
Resistance exercises are ideal for Fours.

Personality Number Four

Four gives the determination to build walls and bridges. It is an even and introverted number, like Two, and expresses itself through its resistance and staying power. Four energy grinds slowly, like the mills of God, and is thoughtful and measured. The other numbers need Four to construct a solid foundation for them, upon which to build their latest ideas and innovations. The Four personality endures change and relies on things that will last forever. Four is the number of reliability and stability. Fours make loyal, dependable, and honourable partners.

83

Personality Three & Four: II

Big spenders
Threes don't need an excuse to spend money; they share their wealth generously.

Three personalities need to stay fit, both in body and mind. Eternally young, even in old age they will enrol in a college course that fires their imagination on their way to pick up their pensions. They are led by the mind and consider practicalities later. Three energy moves very quickly and can leave the rest of us lagging behind. Threes love being surrounded by people of all ages, races, and creeds. This kind of stimulation is food for them. They feed their minds before their bodies and may need to be reminded to eat, shower, and exercise.

Three personalities are delightful to be around, but patience and great forbearance are prerequisites of any potential partner. Threes can spend money like water, but are willing to share it with others.

There is not much that is negative that may be said about Threes as they are such decent people. They can drive themselves too hard perhaps, and sometimes they can talk too much.

Laid-back Fours

Fours are notorious for their slow, patient, and deliberate pace through life. Sensuous and in touch with their appetites, they know exactly what they want to get out of life. They are late developers, but once they learn something, it stays with them forever. They always win a waiting game. Growing Bonsai trees is the perfect hobby for a Four.

They are kind, physical, and tenacious. They respect and honour their marriage vows, which must have been written by a Four. However, they can be controlling, especially of joint finances, and they never overspend. Calm in the face of a storm and protective of their loved ones, whom they may regard as their possessions, Fours prefer a war of attrition to a short battle and have the patience to bear a grudge for years.

On the negative side, Fours can lack imagination and be perfectly happy to watch paint dry. Many Fours have to deal with some kind of health issue – often related to their immobility and lack of flexibility.

Three & Four

Fours make skilled managers of Threes if they work within the entertainment or communication business.

Speaking out
Fives are freedom fighters and designers of social change.

PERSONALITY FIVE & SIX: I Five and Six indicate a shift of emphasis

from the purely personal to a greater social awareness. They are concerned with the larger picture and what they can contribute to improving the quality of life for others. Five is the number of freedom and Six stands for diplomacy and service. They are both extremely creative. Together they offer a vision of a better and more beautiful world that is possible for all of us.

Personality Number Five
Five is the pivotal number where the actual change in attitude occurs. It is odd and outgoing. Personality Fives seem to be positioned between two worlds – their own and that of everyone else. They demand freedom to switch sides and move from one to the other, gathering resources from each. Languages, beliefs and philosophies are their currency and their aim is to set the world free from the bondage of ignorance and prejudice. The weapon they use is humour, and through it, they communicate and enlighten.

The Clown
Fives use humour to challenge the ideas of others.

The lovers
*Sixes are always happiest
when they are in love.*

Personality Number Six

*Six is the number of love, both the love of humanity
and the love of an individual. It is even and
reflective. Sixes need to surround themselves with
people. Their aim is a world where harmony is the
watchword and service the route to it. Sixes
express this higher love through art and creativity.
Six personalities are attuned to beauty and
sometimes addicted to perfection. They express
their aesthetic sense in whatever field they choose
to work in, and excel in diplomacy and arbitration.*

Venus de Milo
*A Six personality would appreciate
this famous sculpture symbolizing feminine
beauty and perfection.*

Personality Five & Six: II

Boldly going
*The great outdoors and the
freedom of wide open spaces
attracts Five personalities.*

Fives love to roam the planet for new experiences. Their search for knowledge and information knows no bounds and they regard the journey itself as being as important as the treasure they seek. Five personalities lead interesting lives and love to recount their adventures, embellishing them with details that match the needs of whoever is listening. Fives are clever. Witty, informative, and mentally alert, they are natural psychologists and scientists. They read other people as easily as they read a book, and have great insight. There are no prizes for guessing that Fives inhabit the world of journalism and mass media. They have a gift for brain-picking and finding the truth. Five personalities soar above specialization and seek the common denominator in all disciplines.

Regarding their negative aspects, Fives tend to skim the surface of life, gathering and collecting useful pieces of information without caring how they get it. Commitment is difficult for them. They can take off into the sunset without a backward glance.

Love all, serve all

Sixes have no favourites and love everyone in the same slightly detached, cool manner. Relationships are necessary for complete happiness and sociable Sixes are not alone for long. In childhood, little Sixes are always accompanied by a best friend. They attract others to them with their magnetic personalities and physical beauty. Six personalities' entire approach to life is artistic and they often use themselves as a canvas upon which to create an image of perfection.

Sixes have a need to be useful and are usually happiest when they are involved in some project or cause. They believe in the power of love and its capacity to heal. Six personalities are gifted healers and carers, and are often found working as health professionals, either in counselling or medical departments.

The negative aspect of this influence means that Sixes sometimes give up their individuality in order to maintain peace and harmony. They often have to fight inertia. Six personalities often push their bodies through extremes to achieve their inner idea of perfection, which may not match reality.

Beauty & Art

Being addicted to beauty, the qualities expressed by Six are those that have been expressed since artists first began to paint – a desire to represent the wonder of the world.

The hand of God
Sevens understand the connection between humanity and divinity.

PERSONALITY SEVEN & EIGHT: I

Seven and Eight take a step towards uniting social development or society with spirituality and power. They are concerned with crossing boundaries – physical, mental, and mystical. This brings up questions about what kind of power is being expressed, and whether it is human or divine. Both numbers work through the interplay of seen and unseen forces, and they attempt to express this to the wider world.

Personality Number Seven

Seven is the mystical number of the monk, the philosopher, the ancient mariner who is always travelling, but never arriving. Seven is odd and active. Sevens have humanity's needs at heart, but prefer the life of the hermit, and to be away from people to ponder and dream. Structuring their insights into a religion, they write inspired sermons and lectures, all aimed at saving us from ourselves. Their breadth of vision is awesome and their gift of oratory charms the birds from the trees.

The monk
Sevens are mystical, philosophical, and reclusive.

Might is right

Like chivalrous medieval knights, Eights will struggle against great odds to achieve their aims.

Personality Number Eight

Eight is the number of power. It contains deep mysteries within its make-up. It is the number of infinity. Eight is even and profound. Many people in the public eye are Eights. They use their personal power to struggle against great odds. Eights are never all that they appear to be. The complexity of the number gives them the urge to overcome, to vanquish, and to lay bare their inner demons. While they do so for their own peace of mind, the result always has wider implications for the rest of us.

Eight

The figure of eight shape is also used to represent eternity.

Personality Seven & Eight: II

Courtly love
Troubadours travelled throughout medieval Europe singing ballads of chivalrous knights and their ladies.

Personality Sevens are continually wandering off. Even when they are present in body, they are often "out to lunch" mentally. They are musical, artistic, and poetic. Like the medieval troubadours singing of chivalry and divine love, Sevens are as much in love with the spiritual as they are with the world of the senses.

The chief preoccupation for Seven personalities is the pursuit of a vision that encompasses and explains everything. They are wise and inspired teachers of the very subjects they are most curious about. The path of wisdom that Sevens tread has no end or boundary, a fact that seems to encourage them to travel. Even in childhood, little Sevens are wise beyond their years.

However, Sevens find it hard to stay focused on the present. Always creating castles in the air and working out how to get there, they find ordinary life confining and may never settle for long.

The master of all he surveys

Brilliant tacticians hell-bent on conquering, Eights are skilled at in-fighting and experts at getting what they want out of life. They often come from a background of struggle. This spurs them on to become captains of industry and heads of government. Machiavellian in their behaviour, they love any kind of intrigue and tend to tackle life head on. Eights have great solidity and balance and do nothing lightly. They are intense and powerful in their ability to stay ahead of the game.

Eight personalities are interested in what makes people tick and make good psychologists and detectives – not because they want to get to the truth, but because they are fascinated by the diversity in human reactions. As children, Eights love excavating the garden to dig up the kinds of things that their playmates run away from.

On the negative side, Eights can be overbearing and unkind. They need an outlet for their power drive. Otherwise, they can become tyrannical schemers and manipulators of those who are closest to them.

Courtly Espionage

Eights display many Machiavellian traits. They would make good spin doctors as they are masters of the art of detection and political game-playing.

91122

NINE, ELEVEN & TWENTY-TWO: I Nine is the completion of the sequence of numbers. It is odd and vital, committed to change, and to wrapping up half-finished projects. Nine is the number that holds the space between the world of today and the world of tomorrow by being an agent of change in the face of stability.

Personality Number Nine

Nine is the point where a change in circumstance occurs. It is odd and self-assertive. Nines fight for what they believe in and are prepared to throw their considerable resources behind a pet project. Philanthropy and creativity go hand in hand in Nines. They are sensitive to the needs of others and practical in their support.

Environmental
Nines are concerned with worldwide issues such as environmental pollution.

Guiding light
Master Numbers act as beacons to light the way in life.

The Master Numbers
Eleven & Twenty-two

These numbers occur infrequently in real life. They are not part of the sequence of numbers in their Master state and so stand outside ordinary behaviour. This is the great responsibility that they carry and it is no wonder that many Master Numbers hide their heads and reduce themselves to Two and Four in everyday life. The Master Numbers are like beacons that light the way to a new level of consciousness, the embryo of which is held within the Two and the Four. It is important to extract the essential meaning of both of these early numbers to understand the esoteric meaning of how the Master Numbers function. The essence of Number Two is Right Relationship and the essence of Number Four is Right Action. It comes as no surprise that many Master Numbers would rather lie low and keep out of the firing line.

Crusaders
Nines are forever on a mission, be it political, humanitarian, or spiritual.

Personality Nine, Eleven & Twenty-two: II

World citizens

Nines are always willing to care for and help others.

Nines are passionate about humanitarian concerns and have great expectations of themselves and others. Their interests are neither personal nor parochial; it is the world that captures them. Whether through politics, religion, or spirituality, Nines try to put right the ills of humanity and are usually knowledgeable about topics like world aid, animal rights, and prison reform. Like the best soldiers, Nines sleep with one eye open. Always on the lookout for any kind of social injustice, Nines will lend their voices and even their lives to higher causes.

Highly creative, Nines always produce art with a sub-text – in the form of paintings, films, and books with meaningful messages – that seek to elucidate and enlighten us on the human condition. Nine comedians make us laugh through our tears.

Nine personalities can, however, avoid emotional commitments by claiming they have their minds on higher things. They can also become obsessive and self-righteous zealots who can kill to prove a political point.

Eleven & Twenty-two

The challenge for Elevens and Twenty-twos is to live up to their potential. Most of us have this problem, but it can become a real struggle for those with Master Number personalities to do so. They often try to fly below cloud cover to avoid being picked up by radar, by simply being ordinary and not drawing attention to themselves.

Elevens can be Twos by being placating and trying to keep everyone happy. Twenty-twos can pretend that they are caught up with their immediate surroundings, but they fool no-one. This occupies them on the outside but is not deeply satisfying. Most Master Numbers spend half their lives keeping their heads down, then must face a crisis.

It may be that all Personality Twos and Fours contain a seed that enables them to act like Elevens or Twenty-twos when things get tough. After all, many people have tapped into extraordinary levels of creativity and spirituality, and they are not all Master Numbers.

Master Numbers

These are relatively rare personality types who, in their early years, pretend to be Twos and Fours before emerging in maturity as world players.

DESTINY NUMBERS

Destiny is your destination on your journey through life. Many people believe that they are no more than a result of their childhood and earliest experiences. Numerology says this is not so; the Destiny, or Life Path, Number demonstrates this. Even if you change your name your Destiny Number never changes. Some numerologists believe that Personality and Destiny Numbers are chosen before we are born so that we will learn certain lessons in this life. The Personality Number is expressed easily and is discernible within our drives and interests. This is not true of the Destiny Number. Our early childhood environment may work against the straightforward expression of our Life Path. It is a difficult tract of life and we struggle through it, developing in the process.

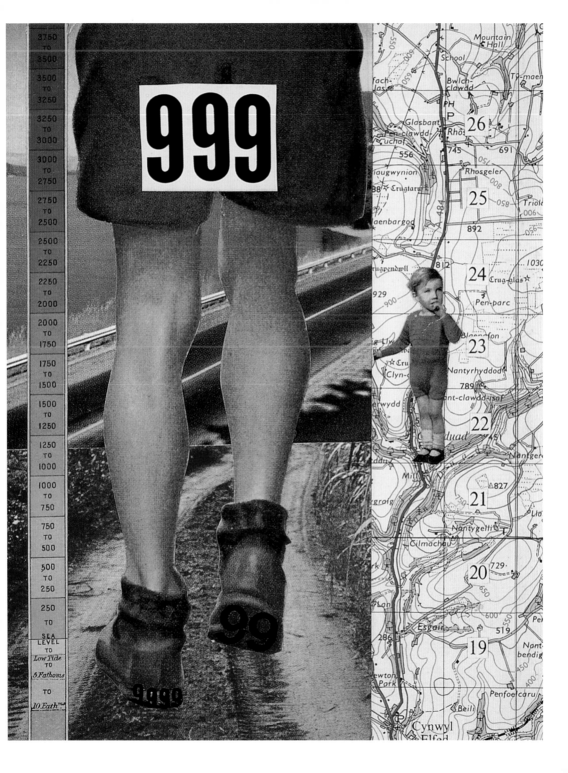

How to Find Your Destiny Number

Remember that, in numerology, you add everything together until you reach a single digit. The exceptions to this rule are the numbers Eleven and Twenty-two.

So, for the Destiny Number, you simply add together the day, month, and year of your birth, and then keep adding until you end up with a number Nine or below. November is the exception to this rule. It always remains an Eleven and never reduces to Two. This means that November is the Master Month of the year and those born during this month have some of its special path to follow.

October is the tenth month and is therefore a compound number. Adding the two digits together reduces it down to One and reflects One's vibrant qualities. However, as it has been combined with Zero it can lend some psychic abilities.

Days
The days of the month all reduce to single digits.

1, 10, 19, 28	all reduce to **1**
2, 20	both reduce to **2**. 11 and 29 remain as **11**
3, 12, 21, 30	all reduce to **3**
4, 13, 31	all reduce to **4**. 22 remains as **22**
5, 14, 23	all reduce to **5**
6, 15, 24	all reduce to **6**
7, 16, 25	all reduce to **7**
8, 17, 26	all reduce to **8**
9, 18, 27	all reduce to **9**

First Example

Our first example is Harrison Ford. He was born on 13 July 1942.

This becomes **13/7/1942**
Add **1** and **3** together (13) = **4** plus **7** (July) = **11**
1942 reduces to **1 + 9 = 10 = 1 + 0 = 1**
4 + 2 = 6
1 + 6 = 7
11 + 7 = 18 = 1 + 8 = 9
This gives a final reduction of **9**
Therefore Harrison Ford has a **Nine** Destiny Number.

You can read the interpretation of this number in the following pages.

Another Example

19 December 1978, which is written 19/12/1978

19 reduces to **1 + 9 = 10 = 1**
December is the twelfth month, so reduces to **1 + 2 = 3**
Therefore 19 December = **1 + 3 = 4**
1978 reduces to **1 + 9 + 7 + 8 = 25** which reduces to **2 + 5 = 7**
The final addition is then **4 + 7 = 11**

Do not reduce this number any further, as it is a Master Number.

Life's adventurer
*Even from early childhood
Ones experience life as
being full of challenges.*

DESTINY ONE & TWO: I The energy of One and Two as Destiny
Numbers packs life with events that make people take responsibility for themselves
and live in harmony with the rest of humanity. They are mirrored by early childhood,
from egocentric infancy to youthful initial attempts to socialize with others. Every Life
Path is like a fractal of the entire range of numbers. Within each is a complete world
of experiences and events which are focused and given colour through the lens of a
particular number.

Destiny Number One
*Number One gives a person the drive to be first and
to lead at every opportunity. One is the number of
the raw ego state of the baby. The One Life Path
ensures that all its needs are met, and guarantees its
survival. Early humankind followed a One Life Path,
hunting for food and competing for the best breeding
partners. Winning was the only option, as losing
meant certain death. Historically, One personalities
may be seen as the hordes of Huns and Goths who
lived by force and destroyed everyone and
everything in their path.*

Learning to care
*Twos often must learn how
to nurture others.*

Destroyers
*Historically, One personalities,
like these Mongol warriors, lived
by force.*

Infancy
*The bond between parent
and child is the basis of the
bond between the individual
and the rest of the tribe.*

Destiny Number Two
*Number Two is the desire to
mediate and placate. Two is the
stage of infancy where the close
emotional union with the mother
is a child's entire world. Early
humankind developed along a
Two Life Path when they began
to plant corn and nurture seeds
all the way to harvest. Social
co-operation meant that more
was accomplished and lives
grew longer. Twos may be
compared to the Minoans who
worshipped the Goddess of
Motherhood and Creativity.*

103

Destiny One & Two: II

Starting out

Ones need to strike out on their own at an early age, for example by joining a youth organization.

Those on a One Life Path are challenged to take control of their own lives and become independent and forceful. Life brings experiences that make them stand up for themselves and banish any cosy thoughts of having a quiet life. The One Destiny offers a school in individual development.

During early childhood, the One Path is usually spent beneath the shadow of events that overtake the family and cause the child to be largely ignored. In order to survive, the child gets the attention he needs by being a helper and putting himself to one side. Looking Destiny in the eye is always dangerous for Ones at the beginning of their lives.

As he matures, his One Destiny ensures that life throws situations at him that force him to come out of hiding and take his place at the head of the queue. Once he takes this step, the One Destiny guarantees that lessons of personal responsibility, self-assertion, and self-reliance lead to the smooth achievement of success and leadership in his chosen field.

Destiny Number Two

The Two Life Path brings many experiences in the art of relationships. Destiny may indicate that relating to others is an innate gift but, for those on this Path of Twos, it is about walking a fine line between union and self-abnegation. This is a delicate balancing act to accomplish, but balance is the key word for the Two Life Path.

The maternal relationship in early childhood is very powerful. The emotionally sensitive Two child finds it hard to separate from this strong bond.

This sets up the Two Life Path's distorted desire for a soulmate who will love him just as his mother did. Life ensures that no such person exists. Two's destiny can force him to play mother to everyone and thus to avoid adult relationships. He may also believe that no-one can love him like his mother.

As Two Destiny matures, he learns not to expect his beloved to fulfil all his needs and desires. He recognizes that he must stand as an equal and take responsibility for his half of all bargains that he makes. Life teaches Twos to appreciate the joy of being part of a twosome and also to have the strength to be an individual at the same time – there is much to be gained from this.

Early Years

The Life Path starts on the day of birth and thereafter it fulfils the destiny contained within each number.

Energy & inertia

Three and Four represent energy and inertia – the twin forces of the Universe.

DESTINY THREE & FOUR: I

The vibrations of Three and Four as Destiny Numbers bring experiences that test individuals in their ability both to expand into life and to contract from it. These numbers represent energies that are polarized, equal in power, and opposite. Like the heartbeat, they open and close, and offer opportunities for people under their influence to control the ebb and flow of their lives. There is an element of control in both of these Destiny paths. Three does it through the mental processes and Four does it through the use of personal power.

Destiny Number Three

Number Three ensures that life is always interesting and tomorrow is even better. It is the path of exploration and being open to new experiences. It is the phase in the life of the child that equates with learning to negotiate with the neighbourhood and to communicate with siblings. The point in the history of the evolution of Western civilization that illustrates this best is the classical period of the early Greeks, with their love of debate and philosophy and their sophisticated development of mathematics.

Destiny Number Four

The Four Life Path brings a test of self-value against a backdrop of apparent scarcity. It is the number of the Earth and being bound in matter. It is the time in infancy when the child learns that the fences around her home keep her in as much as they keep others out, and where discipline is meted out to her. The Roman Empire is an ideal mirror for this Life Path, with its long history of colonization and its use of brute strength to bring the rest of the world to its knees.

Destiny Three & Four: II

New horizons
*Threes find themselves
having to be ready to travel
at a moment's notice.*

The Three Life Path vibration opens the heart, body, and soul to positive experiences and meaningful social activities – or at least that's the theory. In reality, those on this path find it a struggle to dare to believe that life can be that good. Someone with a Three Destiny Number undergoes a lifelong lesson in learning to trust her own mind.

In their early years, Destiny Three children find that they are prevented from exploring their mental abilities. They often have parents who are either scornful of education or limited in their own knowledge and educational backgrounds and so discourage any

attempt their child makes at self-improvement. Some Three Life Path youngsters underachieve for years. However, life being what it is, it eventually throws up opportunities for them to develop their minds, often at the cost of alienation from those dearest and nearest to them.

Later in life, long after school is but a memory, Destiny Threes go out confidently and hungrily into the world to learn on the hoof, travelling and reading, communicating, and experiencing all the bounties that life has to offer.

Destiny Number Four

The vibration of the Four Life Path is dense and moves very slowly. It is designed to bring its owner down to earth. Those with this destiny learn early that if they want anything, they must work for it. Even then, they may have to wait years before they are rewarded. In childhood, Destiny Four's family home may have been financially inadequate. Other siblings may not have felt limited by this want of resources at all, but Destiny Four will have done. The shortage of material wealth somehow translates for her as an inner poverty. This is the Life Path that creates a slow-burning desire for money, and lots of it. The Destiny Four's belief is that assets will make everything all right and that possessions are a measure of their owner's value.

In maturity, the Four Destiny Number leads someone to an appreciation of people and things in their own right, whatever their material worth. These experiences lead to the development of confidence and self-value of a kind that is based on reality. Eventually she finds that she is happier with less material wealth and more emotional contact.

Change & Maintenance

The Destiny Three number brings surprises while Destiny Four is slow and steady. They each learn to take life at their own pace.

Socially aware
Both Fives and Sixes find their lives filled with other people.

DESTINY FIVE & SIX: I The Life Paths of Destiny
Numbers Five and Six offer their bearers the possibility of moving beyond their ordinary expectations. They are filled with experiences that involve large numbers of people. They seek to relate and expand their awareness of the diversity of human behaviour through interaction with humanity. They both need to take others along with them and to show them a better way of living. It is how they do this that marks the difference between these two Life Paths.

Freedom
Fives often spend their lives working for freedom from oppression.

Destiny Number Five
The path of the Destiny Five person lights his yearning for the freedom that knowledge brings. Five is the number associated with the stage of development when a child starts school. He learns about ideas and concepts that are not necessarily the same as those at home and thus gains freedom from family prejudices through education. He also widens his social circle beyond his own level in society. The development of humankind that resonates with the Five vibration is any period of freedom from the slavery of oppressive regimes, like that of the Roman Empire or the African slave trade.

Creative

It is important for Sixes to develop their innate creative abilities.

Destiny Number Six

Destiny Six is the Life Path that leads to the creative expression of love. It is associated with the phase of adolescence when the child begins to feel strong emotional tides within himself and seeks to express them through music and poetry. He worships icons from afar and wants to save the world. The period of human development associated with Six is the Renaissance, with all of its artists, love sonnets, and notions of religious freedom based on a love of humanity rather than archaic rules and lavish courtly behaviour.

Renaissance

The Renaissance in Europe (fifteenth–sixteenth century) was a time of artistic and social freedom.

Destiny Five & Six: II

Powerful ideas

*Fives learn that knowledge
has the power to
set them free.*

Those on the Five Life Path are being encouraged by Destiny to explore the unknown and to leave safety and security behind. Five challenges them to expand their understanding and attitudes to life through their use of the five senses.

In their early years, Destiny Five children are often denied any kind of liberty. They are told what to do, think, and feel by a dominating parent. When they go out into the world, they shrink from taking responsibility for themselves and find situations which keep them trapped. They blame their circumstances rather than admitting their fear of the unknown. Life, however, as always, intervenes by offering them ways of breaking free.

As they explore their own freedom, Destiny Fives realize that freedom should be available to everyone. They learn that it comes in many guises and is a complex concept. Their task is to transmit to others what they perceive about the world around them. Developing good communication skills can help themselves and others. The gift that Five Life Path people have is the ability to teach and broadcast their perceptions to the outside world.

Destiny Number Six

The vibration of Destiny Number Six extends beyond personal concerns into the social arena. Service is the key to this Life Path, and many Sixes are happiest when serving and caring. Six is the number of art and creative expression, so even serving others must be done beautifully. Even if life is lived at the local level, Destiny Sixes are often involved in voluntary work in their community.

Destiny Six children often care for a sick parent or play mother to younger siblings. They are regarded as important by the rest of their family members for their supportive role rather than for their unique creative potential. Young Sixes are artistic and worship beauty. As they grow up, they may deny their inner resources, finding more mundane, everyday chores with which to busy themselves and ignoring opportunities to stretch their talents.

The Six Life Path demands that a balance is struck between the purely functional and the beautiful. In maturity, Destiny Sixes are attractive to others and Life asks them to distinguish between whether they are loved for their outer beauty or their inner qualities.

Pied Piper of Hamelin

This legend is associated with the freedom of Five. The piper promised to free Hamelin of rats, but led away the town's children instead.

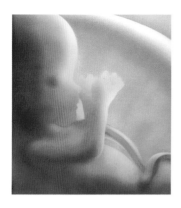

Mystery & wonder
Sevens attune themselves gradually to the mystical realm of life.

DESTINY SEVEN & EIGHT: I The vibrations of Destiny Numbers
Seven and Eight are very different from each other. The energy of the Seven Life Path is diffuse, as if based in another realm beyond the physical world. In contrast to this, the Eight Life Path is rooted in the material world of profit-and-loss and the use of the will. Both Destiny Numbers offer the chance for personal transformation through the letting go of old outworn habits and patterns, which is challenging as well as exciting.

Destiny Number Seven

The Seven Life Path questions assumptions that material reality is all there is to life. The subtle realms of existence are available to Destiny Seven, who needs to express what she knows of them in a way to which the rest of the world can relate. This energy has the quality of antenatal life, when the unborn infant lives in a kind of heavenly state of being without stress or strain from the world outside. The period of human development with a similar vibration is the time Adam and Eve spent in innocence in the Garden of Eden.

Paradise
Destiny Sevens search for their own private Garden of Eden.

The Médicis

Destiny Eight people would relish the powerful wheeling and dealing that took place in the fifteenth- and sixteenth-century Florentine court where Catherine de Médicis (1519–89) played her part in the political intrigues.

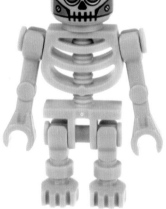

Destiny Number Eight

Life Path Eight creates struggles of a profound nature. Behind them is the impulse that circumstances in the personal life must change forever. The period of development in a person's life that mirrors this path is the point where she crosses over into adulthood and experiences the crisis of identity that accompanies it. The political machinations surrounding the Court of the Médicis in fifteenth- and sixteenth-century Florence reflect many of the qualities of the Destiny Eight person, particularly all the manipulation and power struggles that went on behind the scenes.

Death wish?

Adolescent Destiny Eights may be fascinated by death.

Destiny Seven & Eight: II

Daydreamers

*Sevens often live between
the real world and the world
of their imaginations.*

Life Path Seven is a path into wonderland and the trick is to keep both feet on the ground. The Destiny Number Seven person needs to be devoted to something to which he can dedicate himself and give his time. For many Destiny Sevens, this takes them far and wide, and out into the world for travel and study, preferably alone. The Destiny Seven person has strong intuitive powers which he must trust. In childhood, young Destiny Sevens are the ones gazing out of classroom windows. Being told that their dreams will amount to nothing can wound them deeply and crush their natural wonder about life. They are often drawn to expressing themselves through poetry, mysticism, and music, as expressions of the yearnings that they feel within themselves. When they reach adolescence, Destiny Sevens begin searching for an attachment which could be to a religious figure, a personal relationship, or even a sports team.

Number Seven Destiny energy gives rise to situations that continually expand someone's understanding that there is no single idea, belief, or philosophy that is "the truth". The person under the influence of Destiny Seven learns that there are many truths and ways to express devotion.

Destiny Number Eight

The vibration of the Eight Destiny is dense and slow-moving. It brings lessons and experiences that have a profound effect upon the lives of those under its influence. Eights seem to be tested at every turn to stand up for themselves and their beliefs.

Destiny Eight children are often at the mercy of a bullying parent or teacher, or have to learn survival skills very early. They may have to face the harsh realities of life at a much earlier age than other children. This produces adults who are able to cope in crises and make good leaders. Destiny Eight adolescents are likely to be fascinated by sex, death, and depth psychology, and want to know the answers to the most complex questions.

Those on an Eight Life Path work hard to overcome what they perceive as their inner weaknesses. The lesson that they learn along the way is that they cannot control everything around them and that sometimes things happen in their life without their consent.

The Meaning of Life

Sevens and Eights seek to develop their inner power in different ways — Sevens through their imaginations and Eights through their wills.

9 11 22

NINE, ELEVEN & TWENTY-TWO: I Destiny Nine is the final

number in the sequence and denotes a life of endings and new beginnings. There is a strong sense of Karma in all Nine relationships, as if debts are being paid off or received. Eleven and Twenty-two Destinies are lived out more rarely, due to the hard work involved. The pay-off is huge, however, and can have a far-reaching impact on society.

Destiny Number Nine

The vibration of Number Nine gives someone a strong sense that, in this lifetime, issues that have been carried over from previous lives are finally being resolved and coming to an end. This Destiny Number means that its bearer needs a great deal of energy to bring these matters to a close. Luckily, people with Nine Destinies are filled with enough enthusiasm and zest to go around helping others as well as themselves – to lighten their loads in readiness for the new beginnings that will follow whatever resolutions are coming.

Enthusing others

Destiny Nines are gifted at encouraging others to do their best.

In the spotlight
Nines are attention seekers and like to take centre stage.

Destiny Master Numbers: Eleven & Twenty-two

These two paths vibrate to a very different type of energy from the previous Destiny Numbers. They are rare, especially Twenty-two. It is easy to stray from these paths of Destiny, as they can be so easily reduced to Two and Four. Many people under the influence of these two "Destinies less travelled" prefer to sit back and pretend nothing is happening. These numbers require that people take responsibility for their Destinies. The rewards for their struggle are reflected in their lives, either financially or socially.

Take the high road
Elevens and Twenty-twos take responsibility for their journey on life's road.

Destiny Nine, Eleven & Twenty-two: II

Limelight
Nines often live public lives that bring fame and fortune.

This Life Path almost guarantees to bring those who travel along it into the public eye in some way or another. Many people in show business, for example, are Destiny Nines. They seem to gravitate towards situations that will put them centre stage.

As children, little Nine Destinies are the ones who always notice when the teacher makes an error, and have to point it out. Every misdeed will draw attention and may lead to hours of detention after school. This can create insecurity and the inner belief that they are not as good as the other children in their class. However, their naivety and eternal optimism are rarely completely dimmed and they leap out into life enthusiastically, ready to change the world.

As adults, they believe that life is a process that is not set in stone and that it can be transformed by their actions. This is a Life Path that requires courage from them, and demands that they do not lose sight of their vision.

Destiny Number Eleven

This Master Number ignites the desire to spread the word of humanitarian ideals and shine a light into the dark corners of ignorance. Such a high vibration can have a subtle influence on the daily life of Destiny Elevens. There are many pitfalls along this high road that teaches discrimination and the value of right relationship. It brings out the hidden areas of life – like the occult and mysticism. Whatever subject Destiny Eleven chooses to study, once it is learned, it must be taught to others.

Destiny Number Twenty-two

The Master Twenty-two Life Destiny Number brings a desire to create a solid structure or institution that realizes a dream. This can be anything from a club for street children to a university that teaches citizenship and idealism. Confusing desires for material wealth – an influence brought by the Four Destiny – challenge Destiny Twenty-twos to put the material world firmly in its rightful place, enabling them to use their gains to fund their dreams.

Master Numbers

It is easier for Elevens and Twenty-twos to pretend to be Twos and Fours – if their Destinies will allow them to, that is.

Day numbers
All numbers are reduced to single digits.

DAYS OF THE MONTH: I The numerology of each day of the month is important in the background of the Destiny Number. It forms a basis for the direction taken by an individual's life. The month has a similar numerological meaning that lends weight to a person's Life Path.

Roman calendar
The Roman calendar changed what were originally 28-day months into months of varying lengths; only February retains its traditional number of days. The rest contain either 30 or 31 days. This gives numerologists extra numerals to play with for interpreting the meaning of birthdays and Destiny Numbers.

Moon days
The 28 days of the month relate to the lunar cycle. Literally, month means "moon".

Compound days

All the months contain the reduced numerals 1–9 three times, plus an additional 1, from the 28th day – which reduces to 10 = 1. Some months also have an extra batch of the numerals 2–4 tagged onto the end: the 29th, 30th and 31st. Each numbered day has its own flavour. When the number of the day is a single digit, it encapsulates the pure essence of the number's meaning. So-called compound days are combinations of two single numbers that give the person born on that day the quality of both numbers plus the single one that they reduce to.

Master month

The months also have their numerology from One to Nine, with October and December reducing to One and Three. It is important to note that November falls into the Master Number category, as it is the eleventh month of the year, so is not reduced.

Links

Day Numbers 7 and 16 are linked as they both reduce to the same number.

Days of the Month: II

Your Days are Numbered	
One Days	1, 10, 19 and 28 – all slightly different Ones.
	1 – the prime number, "me first", is fresh and pure initiation.
	10 – Zero lends creative potential to outgoing, initiating energy.
	19 – Nine plus One finishes whatever is begun.
	28 – balances and harmonizes personal power.
Two Days	2 and 20 – two different Twos.
	2 – the pure form of the urge to relate and find a balance.
	20 – Zero gives a creative edge to all relationship ventures.
Three Days	3, 12, 21 and 30
	3 – the pure joy of expansion and communicating.
	12 – the need to balance enthusiasms and personal concerns.
	21 – must be aware of overlooking own needs when caught up with ideas.
	30 – Zero gives a creative aspect to all communication projects.
Four Days	4, 13 and 31
	4 – the sensible, practical outlook.
	13 – outgoing and communicative, with bags of common sense.
	31 – pragmatic information with an idiosyncratic touch.
Five Days	5, 14 and 23
	5 – freedom to express self, easily and joyfully.
	14 – has some limitation of movement, good at planning ahead.
	23 – needs to include others in all ventures and travels.

Your Days are Numbered

Six Days   6, 15 and 24

6 – the lover, the partner, the carer personified.

15 – adds a dash of personal ideas to all relationships and caring for others.

24 – home and domestic life is enjoyed.

Seven Days   7, 16 and 25

7 – the complete dreamer and poet.

16 – actively pursues dreams of a peaceful life.

25 – balances philosophies and reality.

Eight Days   8, 17 and 26

8 – powerhouse of energy to make changes.

17 – personal philosophies help others make necessary shifts in their lives.

26 – nurturing, caring enabler and facilitator.

Nine Days   9, 18 and 27

9 – fights to improve the lot of others.

18 – skilled at moving others through crises.

27 – balances philosophy and humanitarian ideas.

Master Number Days 11, 22 and 29

Master Number days lend illumination and spirituality to all of the person's projects.

THE NUMBERS
OF KARMA

The Karmic, Soul Urge, and Secret Self Numbers are derived from your name. Use the name on your birth certificate and, as an additional influence, any name changes you may have made. You will notice that some numbers are represented many times; these are your Karmic Numbers. They show you what you find easy, and what demands energy from you. The number of the Soul Urge is derived from the total of the vowels in your name. It represents your underlying reason for living. The Secret Self Number is created by the consonants in your name. It represents your will and helps you become a well-rounded individual. The Maturity Number is the sum of your Personality and Destiny Numbers. It represents the overall working-out of your life.

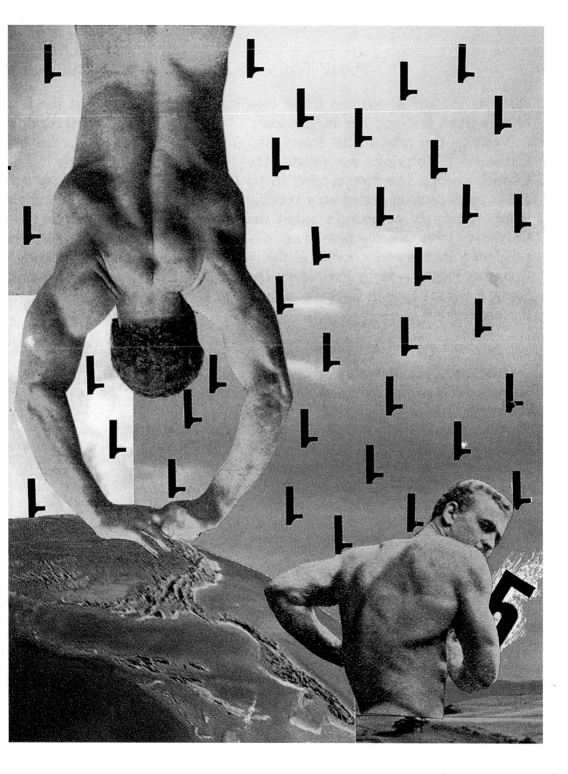

Karmic Numbers

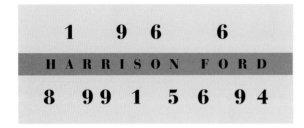

The Karmic Numbers are both those that proliferate and those that are missing from your name chart. These numbers have particular energy patterns. The missing numbers indicate things that seem to slow time down and are hard for you to deal with, while the numbers that repeat frequently indicate things that speed up your life and are fun to work with. Karma consists of both the efforts we have to make in life and the gifts or rewards we bring into the present from the past.

Karma seems a difficult idea for Westerners to understand, but in Eastern philosophies it is regarded as the mainstay of their belief systems. Karma lends a sense of continuity and meaning to our lives, and implies that everything we do has significance in the unfolding

To Calculate the Karmic Numbers

Please refer to the calculation on page 76 using Harrison Ford's name. You will notice that Harrison Ford contains no 2, 3, or 7 as consonant or vowel numbers. So, we conclude that the energies of these numbers are missing from his personality.

Continue with the same name and notice which numbers appear more than others.

1 appears twice, 4 once, 5 once, 6 three times, 8 once, and 9 four times.

Therefore, Harrison Ford's name contains more Sixes and Nines – the other numbers are less prominent.

of our life's pattern. When you have calculated your own Karmic Numbers you will have a clearer idea of the hidden themes that lie within you.

Some people feel that Karma gives only painful lessons, but everything that allows us to become aware of who we are and why we are here can be seen as Karmic. Some people believe that even the animals we care for in this life worked for us in some way in another life. You could work out the numerology of your favourite pets and see if this statement seems reasonable to you.

To Calculate the Number of the Soul Urge

Using the same name chart, calculate the number of Harrison Ford's vowels.

Adding along the top row of both names, they total Master Number Twenty-two, the Builder (Ford first worked as a carpenter on film sets). Twenty-two contains the seed of practical four, the number of realism and material acuity.

Harrison Ford's Soul Urge contained within his name chart is Twenty-two.

To Calculate the Number of the Secret Self

This time add the consonant numbers together. The numbers add up to 51 = 6. Harrison Ford has a Secret Self that is Number Six – the urge to find harmony in his relationships.

Gifts

However much effort is needed to develop it, a spiritual gift gives great joy.

MANY & MISSING NUMBERS: I Some people are gifted
musically, mathematically, or artistically. Other people struggle with the same subjects and, finding them hard, give up. A number that is missing from our Personality Numbers can show what we are looking for in life to make us whole. This can feel like a problem and many people may not be motivated enough to tackle it. However, if we take up the challenge that missing numbers offer, we can achieve more than if we spend time developing our gifts alone. Sometimes, when all the additions are done, the total is the same as the missing number. This indicates that the person must express, through his whole personality, a number that eludes him. The missing number in the name chart may be the Destiny (Life Path) Number. Its qualities bring many possibilities for growth, as it provides insights about Karmic lessons we must encounter. The following section highlights the meaning of missing numbers, and the significance of having many of the same numbers in a name chart.

Gifted

Many personal gifts are expressed through artistic abilities, which in turn give pleasure to others.

Five

A gift for mathematics indicates many Fives occur in the name chart.

Nine

Musicians tend to have Nines in abundance, backed up by Fives.

Many & Missing Numbers: II

An emphasis on one particular number in the name chart suggests a great deal of significance in one area of that person's life. For some people this can be expressed through artistic, technical, or social gifts. For others without the ability to channel the energy, it can be expressed through excessive behaviour patterns that can be difficult for other people to relate to.

The opposite of the emphasized number is the missing number. This can be experienced as a total lack of interest in whatever the number signifies, and often a difficulty in reacting to the number's resonance. It may also lead to an obsession with this area. However, once we meet the challenge of whatever the missing number reveals, we will become empowered and whole.

Significant Numbers

1
Ambition and focus, the drive to achieve and be first. Strong self-belief.

Many – very independent and clear about objectives. Self-expression is easy.

Missing – over-dependent on others. Needs to develop self-confidence.

2
Co-operation, the team player, willing to support and nurture others.

Many – good at partnerships, gives unconditional love and is generous.

Missing – avoids others. Insecure. Needs to learn to trust and be open.

3
Expansion, lust for life, the urge to explore and learn.

Many – enthusiastic, open-minded, optimistic, communicative, fun.

Missing – cold, judgemental, exacting. Needs to nurture a positive attitude.

Significant Numbers

4

Structure, common sense. Pragmatic and realistic. Earthly wisdom.

Many – honest, practical, sensuous with strong physical appetites.

Missing – unable to ground ideas and give them form. Needs to organize life.

5

Freedom of ideas, communication. Friendly, adventurous, and humorous.

Many – intuitive, creative, trusts that life is good. Interested in everything.

Missing – materialistic. Needs to take risks without being attached to results.

6

Balanced, diplomatic, attractive to others, magnetic personality.

Many – caring, loving, cool-tempered and even-minded.

Missing – brusque and uncivil. Alienates others. Needs to learn social graces.

7

Philosophical, kindly, mystical, sensitive, and imaginative.

Many – humanitarian ideals. Sympathetic to all beings. Naturally devoted.

Missing – atheistic, ungenerous towards others. Needs to believe in self.

8

Powerful, courageous, interested in people and their hidden motives.

Many – analytical, psychological, pursues personal transformation.

Missing – powerless, easily led by others. Needs to take responsibility for self.

9

Fighter for ideals, creative, selfless, and charitable.

Many – wants a better world, courageous, interested in public welfare.

Missing – fixed and unchangeable. Avoids opportunities. Must take risks.

Heart numbers
The soul expresses its desires through the heart.

SOUL NUMBERS: I

The Soul Number is derived from adding the vowels in your name chart. The total indicates the most profound reasons for your sojourn on earth. The most esoteric of the core numbers, the Soul Number is a numerical symbol for what your heart desires to express from childhood onwards, as it shows your intrinsic self. It is always interpreted positively because the heart does not make mistakes. If your choices cause you pain, then they are not being made from your heart but from the part of your ego that is designed to teach you something. For instance you may find that your Soul Number is the same as that of someone with whom you have a meaningful relationship, but not necessarily a sexual one; this indicates a karmic bond with that person.

True love

When we are in love we feel healthier than at any other time in our lives. Matters of the heart are at the very root of the Soul Number.

Relationships

We form many loving relationships throughout our lives.

Soul Numbers: II

The Soul Number indicates how we experience and express joy in our lives. It is also the "small voice" within that speaks to us about our true values. It prompts us when we are behaving in a way that takes us away from our true selves. It comes as no surprise to discover that we very rarely listen to this voice.

Each number seeks to reveal the heart's desire in its own way. The impulse behind this, the Soul, is the same for all of us since we are all fragments of the same Divine principle.

All Soul Numbers are compatible with each other – how could it be any other way? If we compare our Soul Number with that of our loved ones, we will discover how we can support each other in new ways, to become joyful and creative Souls.

You may not be aware of your Soul, but it is always there. Some people believe our Souls continue after we die.

This is What Makes Your Heart Sing

1 Your heart desires to shine, to see itself reflected in your lifestyle and in your honesty about yourself. It urges you to stand by your own truths.

2 Your heart desires to share your life with others intimately and lovingly. It urges you to find balance in all things and wishes you to express true values in your relationships.

3 Your heart desires to communicate in a way that enhances your life and the lives of those around you. It urges you to speak positively about the best in everyone.

4 Your heart desires a firm structure within which you can live your life. It urges you to experience the solidity of being on earth and yearns to put its dreams into form.

This is What Makes Your Heart Sing

5 Your heart desires freedom from judgement and conditional loving. It urges you to express yourself openly and honestly and be heard by others who are important to you.

6 Your heart desires beauty and companionship in your life. It urges you to express yourself through your creativity and it yearns for harmony and peace for all beings.

7 Your heart desires the right to dream and express its inner visions. It urges you to merge with a spiritual or humanitarian belief that will nourish it as food nourishes your body.

8 Your heart desires that you listen to it to learn what you really need from life. It urges you to accept that you cannot control everything and that you allow yourself to be an ordinary human being.

9 Your heart desires that you have courage to put into practice the things that you know need to be done. It urges you to be instrumental in creating a better world.

11 Your heart desires that you light the way for others and act as an awakener when everyone around you is falling asleep. It urges you to seek relationships that bring out the highest in everyone.

22 Your heart desires that you build your castles on earth and teach young heroes and gods to spread love and light in the world. It urges you to build a structure that contains the eternal truths.

The will

Secret Self Numbers are linked to the will – the inner engine that drives our lives.

SECRET SELF NUMBERS: I

The Secret Self Numbers are calculated from the consonants in your name. They are most closely linked to your will and the way in which you use it. This is not "willpower", but the kind of will that organizes the core numbers in your life to create an integrated, well-functioning whole. However, the will function described by the consonant numbers is power in action and is easily distorted. You are advised to interpret these numbers with some circumspection as not all interpretations are positive only. Life would never change or improve without will, however. Some words that describe the will are: focused, active, strong, and skilful. People who are high achievers tend to have very strong wills. Sometimes those who seem gentle, mystical, and spiritual have the strongest wills of all, so you need to assess this carefully. When two people have the same Secret Self number, they may be a driving force for change or permanently at loggerheads with each other.

Focus
The purest expression of the will.

Svengali

*The distorted strong will
may attempt to have power
over others.*

Secret Self Numbers: II

The total of the consonants in a name reveals the Secret Self Number, or the will. This can be a contentious area of personal psychology as the will used to be called "willpower", which implied a harsh attitude towards oneself and others.

The will is the engine that drives our lives. It gives us the energy to complete our tasks, to focus on our ambitions and to move mountains if necessary. Without a well-honed will, very little happens.

Sometimes we say we are "going with the flow" which implies that we are being flexible, but it could also signify avoidance, in which case the flow takes us nowhere.

The Secret Self Number can cause conflict in our relationships, or a "clash of wills". Paradoxically, it is this same will that we use to ease the conflicts we encounter, as it is the function that empowers us and enables us to lead creative and rewarding lives.

Will Power

1	Your will energy is focused on getting your needs met; sometimes you ignore the cost. Your Secret Self initiates enterprises that reflect your strength and desire to win.
2	Your will energy is focused on merging with others and may be very manipulative in its action. Your Secret Self forms relationships with others that will teach you about your own motivations.
3	Your will energy is focused on spreading the word, no matter what the content. Your Secret Self energizes communications that stretch your abilities and talents.
4	Your will energy focuses all your thoughts on your personal security, sometimes ignoring new horizons. Your Secret Self works to put your best ideas into form.

Will Power

5
Your will is focused on gaining your personal freedom, while sometimes ignoring your responsibilities. Your Secret Self drives you to teach what you most need to learn.

6
Your will is focused on achieving peace and harmony, sometimes at all costs. Your Secret Self energizes you to create a beautiful environment.

7
Your will energy is focused on living out your dreams, and you sometimes lose touch with reality. Your Secret Self leads you to find a philosophy by which you can live your life.

8
Your will energy is focused on being a catalyst in your environment, often without consideration of others. Your Secret Self plunges you below the surface in order to find the Truth.

9
Your will energy is focused on changing your world, and sometimes makes you into quite a do-gooder. Your Secret Self gives you the opportunity to be active in your community.

11
Your will energy is focused on illuminating the dark corners of life, when sometimes it is best to ignore them. Your Secret Self brings you into contact with the occult and esoteric side of life.

22
Your will energy is focused on the humanitarian issues of life, sometimes at the cost of your personal life. Your Secret Self seeks to align your will with Universal Will.

MATURITY NUMBERS: I The addition of the Destiny Number to the Personality Number produces a total that is known as the Maturity Number. It indicates how your life will work out. If you look at the lives of high achievers, you will notice that who they are is what they do. This number's effects usually show after someone reaches the age of fifty. But of course some people take longer and others reach maturity sooner, as in most things in life. The Maturity Number can be a combination of any two numbers, such as Personality Five and Destiny One, which together make Six, the number of harmony. It brings crisis, through numbers One and Five, into the person's life until they learn to balance their inner conflicts. To ensure that you fulfil your potential, your Maturity Number must turn up somewhere else in your name chart. A relationship with someone whose numbers reflect your Maturity Number will also kick-start the unfolding of your life's purpose.

The Magician

As the Magician Tarot card indicates, the power to be effective is a gift that comes with maturity.

True adulthood
Retirement can be the most satisfying period of our lives.

Careful
Maturity number Nines have caring natures which make them ideally suited as welfare workers and carers.

Maturity Numbers: II

The following numbers are totals of two other digits. The effects of the two component numbers can be discerned by reading the previous sections on Personality and Destiny Numbers. Maturity Numbers indicate a way of harmonizing and blending the two vibrations.

Sometimes both components of the Maturity Number can indicate a harmonious and steady path through life. One and Three, for example, are similar and can indicate a life where success as a writer or broadcaster can continue into later life. They result in Maturity Number Four, which may offer financial security.

Two very different energies are self-motivated One and team-spirited Two. A game of tennis, in which two individuals play together yet against each other, describes them well. They make Maturity Number Three, which indicates a later career in coaching or teaching.

Maturity

1 **The late developer.** You are someone who slowly climbs to the top of the ladder. Nothing will knock you off-track once you get there. Individuality based on experience.

2 **The skilled mediator.** Life gives you many insights into the hidden dynamics of relationships. One special relationship teaches you more about yourself than you could imagine.

3 **The experienced communicator.** You learn all the tricks in the trade to get your message across. As you mature, you become more optimistic and trusting of life.

4 **The practical idealist.** Life forces you to root all your ideas in solid ground. In your later years, you will have accumulated a solid body of experiences to put into whichever form you choose.

Maturity

5   **The detached observer.** You gain freedom from your inner conflicts. Your travels through life enable you to recognize that real freedom comes from within yourself and is never based on outside circumstances.

6   **The well-balanced personality.** Life gives you the opportunity to gain skills which lead to personal growth. You offer these to others who are in times of difficulty, as you have the wisdom to know what and how to give people what they need and what is most useful to them.

7   **The realistic dreamer.** The search for spirituality gives you a boundless, generous philosophy regarding human nature. Your devotion to your ideals teaches you that Truth takes many forms. You develop the ability to live in the world without being overly attached to it.

8   **The skilled investor.** Experiences force you to take your life into your own hands. No-one will do what you have to do for you. Life shows you how to channel your energies so that they become an effective tool.

9   **The welfare worker.** Your humanitarian goals become easier to attain as you mature. Others become more sympathetic to your ideals as you learn to detach from your intensity.

11   **The Magician.** Life gives you many opportunities to take responsibility for your psychic gifts. The choice is yours. The greyer your hair, the more people value your insights.

22   **The Master Mystic.** Life offers you the possibility of building something that will outlast you. It may have enormous potential for good in the world. Your challenge is to dare to believe it.

PERSONAL HARMONY & SPIRITUALITY

Psychologists and marriage therapists acknowledge that the basis for any meaningful relationship starts with the one you have with yourself. Numerology gives you a head start in the intimacy stakes if you understand the significance of your core numbers and what they represent in your life. Within your personality, every number has a personality of its own, each with its own needs and drives. Problems arise when the different personalities all demand your attention at the same time. The trick is to make them all play the same tune to the same rhythm, like the most well-rehearsed orchestra. Some numbers relate better than others and bring about inner harmony. Others cause turbulence and stress. This leads to inner unrest or "divine discontent" and drives us to search for answers to the big questions in life.

Your Inner Relationship

Making it real
*The numbers come alive when they
are applied to your life.*

The best way to begin to unravel the complex threads of what looks like a labyrinth of numbers is to look at an example. We cannot analyse the information about Harrison Ford here as, though he is "known" to many people, we do not have his permission. You may have a go yourself, however.

Jayne is a naturally cheerful Seven Personality. She is interested in exploration, both mental and physical. She is stimulated by new ideas and philosophies. New ways of living and different cultures interest and excite her passions. Life will always work well for her; although as both her Soul Number and Will Numbers are Eight, life will not be without its challenges. Perhaps the most important journey she will make will be to search deeply within her own psyche to uproot stultifying habits. Jayne is determined to make those changes in her being which will inevitably impact on her chosen life path. She works hard to overcome outworn patterns, has undergone psychotherapy, and studies various mystical subjects.

The missing even numbers Two, Four, and Six imply that she needs to find balance in her life and take a dispassionate view of things. Jayne says she is very enthusiastic about her interests (Personality Seven) and is an all or nothing person. Destiny Number Three combines with Personality Seven to make a pioneer and innovator in her life. Maturity Number One ($3 + 7 = 10 = 1$) implies that she will create something uniquely her own.

Harrison Ford

Birth date: 13 July 1942
Personality Number –1
Soul Number – 22
Destiny Number – 9
Secret Self (Will) Number – 6
Many – 6 and 9
Missing – 2, 3, 7
Maturity Number – 1

Jayne Lisa Harris

This is the name chart of a client of mine who has given her permission for me to use her data in this book.

Birth date: 6 December 1974
Personality Number –7
Soul Number – 8
Destiny Number – 3
Secret Self (Will) Number – 8
Many – 1 – she has 6, in fact
Missing – 2, 4, 6 –
note that they are even numbers.
Maturity Number –1

Prediction & Timing

The section on prediction and timing of events will continue Jayne's story and show how her numbers have blossomed in her life.

Individuality
The assortment of numbers makes each of us special and unique.

COMBINATIONS ONE TO FOUR: I

There are seven categories to consider when analysing a name chart. Each number has a need to express itself, and a combination of such expressions makes our individuality. Numbers One to Four are straightforward energies. They represent the four elements – Fire, Water, Air, and Earth – and the four directions – North, South, East, and West. This section describes the relationships between numbers. These are not categorized as having functions, e.g., as Soul Numbers, but simply as number combinations. Refer to previous pages to deepen your sense of how they function in a name chart. Learning the nuances between Soul Numbers and Secret Self Numbers becomes easier if you think of them as Heart (Love) and Will energies. You can then interpret the Soul Number lovingly with your heart and the Secret Self Number more rigorously with your will. Remember, a combination of two numerical energies is not the same as the total when the numbers are added together. Consider the form their union takes, not the total number they make.

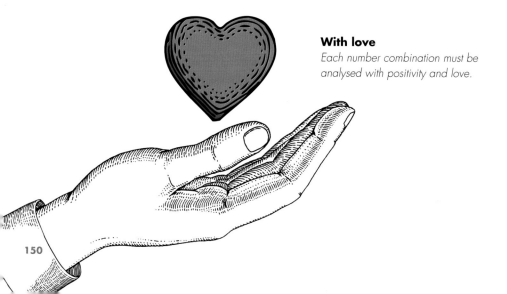

With love
Each number combination must be analysed with positivity and love.

Foursomes

There is a correspondence between the four elements and the four directions.

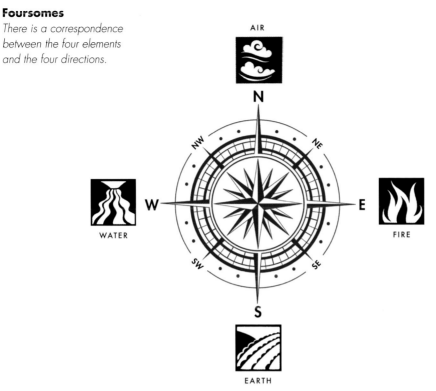

AIR

N

NW

NE

W | E

WATER | FIRE

SW

SE

S

EARTH

Inner union

The two halves of the brain interpret two separate realities: the material and the intuitive.

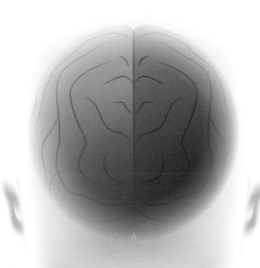

Combinations One to Four: II

Niccolò Machiavelli

*He typified a combination
of Three with Eight.*

These charts indicate how combined number principles can work together in one person. Many number combinations have both positive and negative meanings. As you become familiar with them you will also be able to add your own insights. All the numbers in the name chart combine differently, depending on the nature of each individual number. Practise on those closest to you to widen your knowledge and develop your intuition.

One – The Urge to Act Combines with:

One	Double action and total focus, or too much ego-directed force.
Two	Combines ego-drive with compassion, or makes for indecision.
Three	Combines action and the transmission of information. Over-talkative.
Four	Can result in measured action or a build-up of inner frustration.
Five	Urge for freedom. Passionate about ideas or could be over-subjective.
Six	The drive for perfection. Creative. Can be indulgent and complacent.
Seven	The eternal student. Can spread self too thinly. Escapist.
Eight	The urge to pull down and build up. Can overdo power drive.
Nine	The social activist. Pursues ideals. Can become a political bore.

Two – The Urge to Relate Combines with:

Two	Double intensity of relationship urges. Can be too conciliatory.
Three	Uses words to reconcile and balance. May manipulate verbally.
Four	The home-maker. These two static energies dislike and avoid action.
Five	Needs emotional freedom. Struggles with commitment to loved ones.
Six	The caretaker and healer. May look for perfection in relationships.
Seven	Worships loved ones. May fall in love with unattainable people.
Eight	Attracted to powerful partners. May manipulate emotionally.
Nine	Believes strongly in ideals. Gives all to the struggle for a better world.

Three – The Urge to Communicate Combines with:

Three	The traveller or teacher. Spreads the word and may gossip.
Four	The writer who puts words into form. Can be tongue-tied or stutter.
Five	Freedom of information. Powerful but needs compassion. Arrogant.
Six	Beautiful words – the poet. Harmonious voice. Troubadours, messengers.
Seven	Able to express dreams verbally. Science fiction or fantasy writer.
Eight	The propagandist, spin doctor. Sharp wit. Machiavellian and scheming.
Nine	Lively thinker and communicator. May get into verbal fights.

Four – The Urge Towards Structure Combines with:

Four	Sets everything in stone. Can be immovable and solid. May be bigoted.
Five	Union of concrete and abstract ideas. Imaginative teacher. Writer's block.
Six	Sensuous healer or chiropractor. Puts beauty into form. The sculptor.
Seven	Practical idealism. Travels the earth in search of mystical visions.
Eight	The banker. This combination can become very stuck in matter. Snobbish.
Nine	Structures the urge to change the world. The soldier, the freedom-fighter.

The Chakras

These are energy systems within the human body. The functions described by each Chakra relate directly to the symbolism contained in numbers One to Seven. Chakras are known by their numbers rather than their position, for example: the second Chakra.

COMBINATIONS FIVE TO NINE: I A number occurring many
times in a name chart will amplify the particular aspects it represents. Missing numbers make whatever they help to happen difficult to achieve. Remember that these are called Karma Numbers, so their vibrations are important for general happiness. The numbers Five to Nine vibrate with progressively more subtle energies. Five inspires abstract concepts, while Nine brings them to completion. Since all of these energies are present within a person's life, it is apparent how we become such complex, interesting people. No one is composed of just a single number. No matter how many examples of a particular number someone may have in his name chart, other numbers present will affect its impact. Although some people may behave like one number, this actually indicates that their energy is blocked, and they are unable or unwilling to stimulate it. It can be part of the numerologist's work to facilitate or awaken the shifting of stuck energy.

The mystic's dream

Search for inner peace and harmony by finding balance between the Chakras.

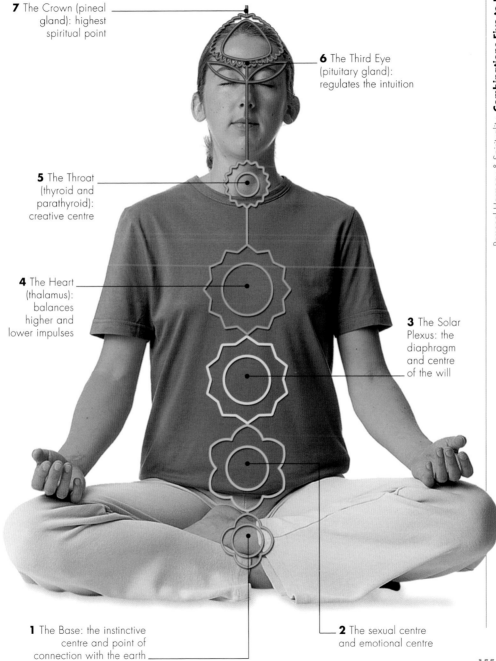

7 The Crown (pineal gland): highest spiritual point

6 The Third Eye (pituitary gland): regulates the intuition

5 The Throat (thyroid and parathyroid): creative centre

4 The Heart (thalamus): balances higher and lower impulses

3 The Solar Plexus: the diaphragm and centre of the will

1 The Base: the instinctive centre and point of connection with the earth

2 The sexual centre and emotional centre

Combinations Five to Nine: II

Peace
*Outer stillness reflects
an inner calm.*

The Master Numbers usually remain as Two and Four in early life. They emerge gradually in late adulthood, when a person is well-established in life and is in a position to be effective with the Master vibrations.

Eleven makes its presence felt as an impulse to illuminate and alert humanity to the esoteric levels of life.

Twenty-two lends impersonal ambition and a desire to implement social reform programmes to whichever numbers with which it combines.

Inner harmony and spirituality

The numbers Five to Nine are the social numbers, implying an impulse to work with and for others. The two Master Numbers go beyond the social into the political arena so they need to take great care how they express the other numbers in their profile.

In the past this kind of information was taught only in mystery schools, but nowadays these secrets are available to us and offer the possibility of self-understanding and empowerment.

Inner harmony comes from recognizing and accepting the various energies that make up your character. This harmony may be compared to an orchestra; the conductor brings the players together in harmony. Once you are able to harmonize the different energies within yourself, you experience wholeness and inner health. This level of being is your natural right, although some people perceive it as having a mystical quality.

Five – The Urge for Freedom Unites with:

Five | The joy of exploring ideas. Freedom and knowledge. Mental exhaustion.

Six | The art historian or critic. Balanced ideas. Over-critical and perfectionist.

Seven | The cosmic cowboy. Devoted to ideas. The seeker of Truth.

Eight | Powerful life-changing concepts. Psychoanalysis. Propaganda.

Nine | Acts out humanitarian political ideals. The freedom-fighter or terrorist.

Six – The Urge for Harmony & Beauty Unite with:

Six | The arch mediator. Beauty and healing combine. Addiction to perfection.

Seven | Belief in harmony and goodwill to all. Devoted lover.

Eight | Transforming power of love. The courtesan. Money for love.

Nine | Balance between action and idealism. Upsets balance for effect.

Seven – The Urge for Idealism Unites with:

Seven | Armchair traveller. Exploration and crossing boundaries. Escapism.

Eight | Belief in materiality. Realistic. Can be atheistic and cynical.

Nine | The reformer. Devotion to highest ideals for humankind. Unrealistic.

Eight – The Urge for Profound Change Unites with:

Eight | Extremely strong will. Resists changes in self, not in others. Wilful.

Nine | Will in action for social change. Abrupt endings. Destructive.

Nine – The Urge for Social Idealism Unites with:

Nine | Focused on social and group concerns. Personal life ignored.

COMPATIBILITY IN RELATIONSHIPS

Numerology enables us to see how people will relate to each other and what they will gain from their relationships with others in various walks of life. There are many ways of relating to others. We have relationships with our parents, friends, bosses, even with the dentist. However, we do not relate to them all in the same way. Numerology shows you why people are married or living with a partner whom you would not have chosen for them. You may not be privy to the dynamics of their personal intimacies and will not see what is really going on between them. However, when you study the way their numbers are arranged, you begin to see in what ways they are fulfilling each other's needs.

Jayne's Relationship

Numbers in love
Certain numbers find some other numbers irresistible – just like people.

The basis of understanding is the acceptance that we are all different and have different needs. Every relationship brings us something – an experience, a lesson, or even the determination not to do something again. It is as if we are all signposts for each other's growth and development – pointing towards the uncovering of talents and Karmic bonds.

In any relationship, there are two people involved. However, numerology tells us that beneath the surface, things are much more complicated. Every name chart contains many different numbers and each number makes its own demands upon a relationship.

Weighing the evidence

Jayne Lisa Harris, our earlier example, is a Personality Seven and Destiny Three. Although her Personality Number includes an Eight, her name is almost exclusively made up of the odd numbers, many of them Ones. She is missing Two, Four, and Six (see page 149). So what numbers will her Higher Self draw her to, so that she may gain wholeness, health, and happiness?

Jayne's husband's name chart (data withheld for confidentiality) contains Personality One and Destiny Eleven (or Two). They were married for a number of years.

His Personality One encouraged Jayne to be independent and to follow her own interests. His Soul Number is Eight which lent weight to the Eight in Jayne's numbers, so although they shared desires in common, it proved too heavy for them both to deal with ultimately and they separated.

His Secret Self Number is Two and Jayne's is Eight. This is challenging for them both, because each finds it difficult when the other asserts their strong will. In any kind of battle, Eight can out-manipulate Two, but not without a communication breakdown resulting in many brooding silences.

Jayne's Maturity One and her husband's Maturity Three combine to make Four. This offered a good family structure within which to raise children. However, the strength of Jayne's Personality Seven proved too independent for her to stay in the marriage. This has set them both free to develop their creativity in new ways.

Relating with Numbers

Compatibility is easy to read with numerology. A close study of the charts of both people in the relationship will explain why they are attracted to each other.

Bliss

Understanding our compatibility with other numbers helps us understand why that one person is so special in our lives.

RELATING: ONES & TWOS

Ideally matched, One is outgoing, initiating, and full of self-confidence, while Two reflects the energy of others, is more careful and thoughtful. Two says, "you first," which is fine for One, who thinks in terms of "me first". Actually, it suits them both. This is an example of an ideal or archetype. Same-number people also find each other very attractive because their vibrations are familiar. Two Ones usually have a sporty, active, energetic marriage – fun as long as goals are shared. Similarly, Twos often find other Twos to stay at home with, and reflect each other in an endlessly repeating, loving loop. This is fine so long as they free themselves periodically from their fascination for each other. Twos can be a little like "Babes in the Wood" who spend the rest of their lives wandering around together.

Energetic Ones
Competing against each other can be a great aphrodisiac.

Two Ones

This relationship can be fun as long as goals – like the next mountain to be climbed or the next million to be made – are shared.

Peaceful Twos

A life of calm and nest-building suits Twos.

Relationships: Ones & Twos

Togetherness
Some numbers fit each other naturally while others need a little more effort.

In all their relationships, Ones promise excitement, activity, physical passion, and fun. With Threes, Ones can go into orbit. Ones find Fours sensuous, but may feel slowed down by them. With Fives, they are intense and argumentative. With Sixes, friendship and sharing go hand in hand. Ones can relate to Sevens as long as they stick around. With Eights, they have power battles. They find Nines stimulating but not interested enough in personal concerns.

In business, the snappy, upwardly mobile One may find a Two personal assistant to be a very supportive team player and co-operative back-up player in difficult times.

Work relationships for Ones are fine so long as there is enough space for them to move around freely and to be spontaneous. A Four boss may limit but teach One self-control. On the whole, however, Ones are happier if they are self-employed and have a staff made up of Twos and Sixes.

As parents, Ones need to learn tolerance for any little number who does not inherit their zest for life.

Twos & relating

In business, the intuitive, sensitive Two may find a One sales manager a talented asset in any business. Twos are supportive of their colleagues and always remember birthdays and anniversaries. However, Three or Five bosses may value intellect over intuition and leave Twos feeling undervalued. Two and Four might run a successful family business together.

In all relationships, Twos are emotional, sensitive, and think before they express themselves. With Threes, they are expansive and enjoy travelling. With Fours, they can be physically affectionate and build a home. With Fives, too many words and not enough emotions are in the relationship. With Sixes, sharing and creating beauty predominate. With Sevens, Twos may limit their emotional expression. Eights may prod the sensitivities of Twos and hurt them. Nines encourage them to be nurturing.

As parents, Twos need to learn to let go and allow their offspring to take risks without instilling fear into them.

Mix and Match

Relating is an art and many of us find it takes lots of practice. Those who do find it easy make good relationship counsellors.

RELATING: THREES & FOURS

Three and Four are totally different in their expression and response to life. Threes are expansive and need to live life to the full. Fours need to be careful and in control of their resources. When Threes play piano, they use all the notes and the chords; Fours play *Chopsticks* with two notes at a time in their minimalist way. Any conflicts between them may be worked out in the way they handle their finances. Threes spend and Fours save. Threes in a relationship with each other can mean a lot of air tickets and passports. They find each other mentally stimulating and can stay awake for hours discussing the meaning of life. Their home life can be a showcase for their love of other cultures. Fours often find each other too structured and stubborn. Their relationships always have a strong flavour of business about them as they have a need for security and a desire to invest in property. Fours often marry late in life for economic rather than emotional comfort. They could run a business or an estate together. Sometimes Fours live side by side having little contact with each other.

Culture vultures
The home life of Threes will expand the minds of all who share it.

Calm landscape
*Fours look for this kind of serenity
in their relationships.*

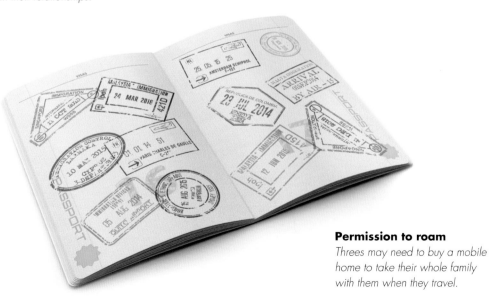

Permission to roam
*Threes may need to buy a mobile
home to take their whole family
with them when they travel.*

Relationships: Threes & Fours

Growing together
Fours will tend their families as lovingly as they tend their gardens.

The kind of relationship Threes and Fours will have together has been covered on the previous page. They are better in business together than they are in marriage.

Threes offer a mentally stimulating and life-broadening experience to others. They are witty, easy-going, and lively. Threes find Twos nice to come home to. Sixes help them entertain their many diverse acquaintances without batting an eyelid. With Nines, they produce creative ventures that set the world on fire. With Fives, Threes may be last seen packing for the Andes, if they can stop talking long enough.

At work, Threes are happiest in the translation department or wining and dining foreign visitors. They find a Four boss too narrow in approach; Four may drive Three to find another job or into freelancing. An Eight accountant could be helpful in sorting out their finances.

As parents, Threes may read their children Norse and Greek legends well before they start school, but overlook regular mealtimes. And they may not notice untidy hair or missing buttons.

Fours & relating

In all relationships, Fours are sensual, steady, and reliable. With Fives, they can feel that they have to run to keep up. With Sevens, Fours may experience the sensation of sailing in a leaky boat. Fours usually speak a different language from the emotional numbers Two, Seven, and Nine, teaching them new approaches to life. Fours have solid friendships with Sixes that may outlast any romance.

Reliable, honest, hard-working, and quietly ambitious with long-term goals, Fours need to be surrounded by numbers that shake them out of their ruts. Threes will suggest foreign expansion, and Twos will successfully negotiate a merger with them if Fours will allow it. Fives do not sit still long enough for Fours, but they are filled with bright, creative ideas.

As parents, Fours enjoy physical activities with their children, like looking after animals, gardening, and hill-walking. They encourage their children to save their pocket money.

Rock Solid

Fours are unshakeable when they give their hearts. They offer balance and solidity to a relationship and are never "here today, gone tomorrow" types.

RELATING: FIVES & SIXES

Five and Six relate through their social antennae. Outgoing Five is the number that spreads the word and therefore craves an audience, while magnetic Six attracts through beauty, honesty, and people skills. Both numbers are able to allow their partners to do their own thing and live independent lives. Together they can form a relationship that is romantic, stimulating, and has the potential for deepening into true friendship. Two Fives in a relationship together will enjoy getting out and about. They will know the best watering holes and restaurants in their neighbourhood. Whenever they go out, they will rarely be alone, as they tend to know everyone, and always gather a group around themselves. Active discussion and lively debates are lifeblood for Fives. Sixes are friendly towards everyone and are archetypal lovers. Romantic, sensual, and sensitive to the needs of others, Sixes love being in love. Their lives are spent being good partners in whatever type of relationship they find themselves. They can be cool and reserved, though. It is the idea of love rather than passion that turns them on. Sixes together have a marriage that enables them to venture out into the world. With Fives, they find even more possibilities available to explore together.

Food-lover
Social Sixes enjoy mixing with people in large numbers.

Dinner for Six
*Exotic foods and fine wines are
always on the agenda for Sixes.*

Language of flowers
*Sixes never forget to give
flowers on the right occasion.*

Restaurant explorer
*Fives enjoy sharing foreign
foods with their partners.*

Relationships: Fives & Sixes

Freedom
*Relating to a Five can mean
that life is never predictable and
is always stimulating.*

In all their relationships, Fives need to keep mental stimulation and verbal communication going. Their priority in any relationship is that other people will communicate back. Nothing scares Fives more than stony silences.

Three partners sometimes stray too far from the beaten track for the comfort of Fives, although they like to hear about it later. Fives like a compass and map when travelling, and find the imprecise directions which Sevens give confusing. Fives and Sevens sometimes seem to talk two different languages. There can be financial struggles and arguments between Fives and Eights about who holds the purse strings and why.

At work, Fives keep everyone informed about what is going on. Four bosses can rely on the mental agility and creative ideas of Fives. With Nines, Fives can create a good fund-raising programme to implement in their community. With Ones, they can launch active weekends for colleagues.

Five parents can stimulate their children's interest in almost anything. However, Fives may have difficulty understanding a child who is more private and introverted than they were.

Six & relating

Sixes love the first stages of a love affair, and are good at relating. They will always find a middle ground where both people get what they need from each other. In all their relationships, Sixes are fair-minded, cool and even-handed. Sensual and sensitive to the needs of their lovers, Sixes are friendly towards everyone and are equally happy in relationships with Sevens, Nines, and Twos. Threes may be problematic as their enthusiasms are not refined enough for Sixes, but Eights have the right amount of sensible passion.

Sixes enjoy working in areas of health and beauty, where their friendly manner is an asset. They particularly enjoy working for Four and Eight bosses, and appreciate the broad humanitarian vision of Nines.

Six parents crave beautiful children and care about appearance and clothes. They may even push their offspring into modelling or stage school.

The Art of Loving

Sixes raise relating to a high level of accomplishment. They are gifted in the sensual arts and know how to prevent their lover's interest cooling off.

SEVENS, EIGHTS & NINES

The three final numbers in the sequence are looking for something more out of their relationships than just home cooking and hand-knitted socks. They are all concerned with life within a bigger picture and look for partners who complement that. Many Sevens and Nines are filled with "divine discontent" and are natural wanderers. Home is wherever they happen to be and they are not possessive of their loved ones. Their expectations of their relationships are as easy-going and open-ended as they are. Sevens usually prefer to be alone for long periods of time, which can be tricky for their partners. Nines may love their pet projects more than another person, so Seven and Nine can "mix and match" happily with each other. Eights, on the other hand, are passionate, intense, and possessive of their loved ones. When Eights say "my wife/husband", the emphasis is on the possessive. When two Eights get together, the earth really does move. If they subsequently separate, the knives can be out for a very long time. Eights need to be in control and hold onto their chequebooks very tightly.

Culinary delights
Not on the menu for the partners of Sevens and Nines, but Eights will produce excellent meals.

Seven's motto
"Wherever I hang my hat is home."

Cosy
Sevens and Nines don't crave home comforts as they are natural wanderers.

Sensual Eights
Eights are definitely bath people rather than shower people. They love to linger and relax rather than refresh themselves quickly.

175

Relationships: Sevens, Eights & Nines

Thrifty

Frugal Eights like to keep their wallets firmly closed.

Loneliness is not a sufficient reason to motivate Sevens into relationships. They fall in love only if they believe that their beloved is a divine, rather than a human being. In love, they experience the expansion of their souls and touch the heart of the Universe. The poetry and music that result are truly inspired. When they find out that their loved one is only human after all, they start packing for their next lonely trek to some other far-off land. Sevens can be happy with any of the other numbers. They probably would not notice any shortcomings in their partner because they live in their dreams most of the time and rarely touch the earth. They are happiest working alone, creating and developing their personal dreams.

As parents, they can enter a child's world and be truly magical.

Eight & relating

Eights are driven by their passions and ambitions to choose a partner for life. Note that there is an emphasis on "life" here. They are powerful and successful people who want the perfect accessory in a mate. Eights always have money, but do not part with it easily, even when in love. So partners be warned.

Magnetic Eights have a profound effect on others. Sevens very much irritate Eights with their airy-fairy ways, and they cannot control Ones. Twos, Fours, and Sixes are best suited to them. As parents, Eights want to be able to give their children everything that they lacked in their own childhoods.

Nines & relating

Nines need a helpmate to stand beside them while they save the world. They are attracted to a partner who shares their social objectives, political affiliations, or spiritual ideals. They are passionate about life and their ability to change things – so partners beware.

Nines are good with "get up and go" numbers, but find Fours and Eights too cautious and conservative for them. An Eight could fund a project, however, and make a good business partner.

As parents, Nines prefer teenagers to babies. They enjoy taking their youngsters to rallies and debates.

Isn't Love Wonderful?

Sevens and Nines often choose partners from different cultural or religious backgrounds to their own. Eights often marry the girl-next-door.

PREDICTION

Once all your core numbers are in place, you can begin to take steps into the world of prediction. Numerology tells you what energies will be influencing you over certain periods of time – including yesterday and today, as well as tomorrow – although it will not tell you exactly the form the energies will take as they work through your life. There are three categories in this section: Pinnacles, Challenges, and Personal Years. The techniques for calculating these are not difficult to master. The first two techniques are similar to progressions in astrology and relate directly to calculations made from the core numbers. They resemble an unfolding of potential within your personality and are symbolic in nature. The Personal Year moves with you, moment to moment.

Pinnacle Numbers: I

Healer
*Jayne will pursue a career
in alternative medicine
for many years.*

We have four Pinnacle Numbers in our lives. Each Pinnacle represents a period that has a distinct keynote. These numbers indicate how and when your potential will work out and shows what you can do to facilitate the process. Each Pinnacle Number lends a distinct atmosphere, but the details of each period are not predictable.

To calculate Pinnacle Numbers

The first and last Pinnacles are the longest periods. The middle two last nine years each. The fourth period is open-ended; it has no end-date.

The first Pinnacle Number begins at birth but does not end at 18 years old. If it did we would have very short lives. The length of the first period is always calculated from 36 years.

Subtract the Destiny Number from 36 years to find the length of the first Pinnacle. In Jayne's case, this is 36 minus 3 (Destiny Number) = 33. So her first Pinnacle ends at age 33. Jayne's Pinnacle

Pinnacle Calculation Table	
Example: 6 December 1974 (Jayne's birth date) = **Destiny Number 3**	
1ST PINNACLE	birth day plus birth month = 6 + 12 = 18 = **9**
2ND PINNACLE	birth day plus birth year = 6 + 3 = **9**
3RD PINNACLE	combination of 1st and 2nd Pinnacles = 9 + 9 = 18 = **9**
4TH PINNACLE	birth month plus birth year = 12 + 3 = 15 = **6**

Numbers are unusual because her first three periods – up to the age of 51 – are all ruled by the same number. This indicates a destiny involving healing and idealism. She has already made the choice to pursue a career in alternative medicine during her first Nine Pinnacle, so we can assume that these studies will intensify as she matures. She will be focused on fulfilling her ambitions.

Unlike Jayne, most of us have different Pinnacle cycles. It may be useful for you to calculate these numbers for people who have lived through the first three cycles. Find out how they responded to each new Pinnacle number, particularly during the change-over periods. Then you can begin to predict for others.

Jayne's Pinnacles are:	
1ST PINNACLE	0–33 years = 9
2ND PINNACLE	33–42 years = 9
3RD PINNACLE	42–51 years = 9
4TH PINNACLE	51 onwards = 6

PINNACLE NUMBERS: II

Pinnacle Numbers are linked to your Destiny Number and help you realize your potential. Your Pinnacles show you how to bring hidden qualities into form during four distinct periods, based on nine-year cycles. The first and last Pinnacles are the longest periods, the middle two run consecutively for nine years each, and the fourth Pinnacle has no end-date. The length of your first Pinnacle, which begins at birth, is calculated by subtracting your Destiny Number from 36. This number represents the age at which you will change over to your second Pinnacle. Please note that the numbers One to Nine do not run in sequence because each Pinnacle is calculated separately using various components of the Destiny Number (see pages 180–1). The same number can appear more than once during the four periods. Master Number Pinnacles are possible and can indicate periods of intense consciousness-raising and mystical development. In some cases, especially if they appear as First Pinnacles, life may follow their reduced Two or Four vibration as Master energies may be difficult for a young person to express.

Pinnacle Numbers
Pinnacle Numbers offer us the opportunity to reach our highest potential as we travel on life's journey.

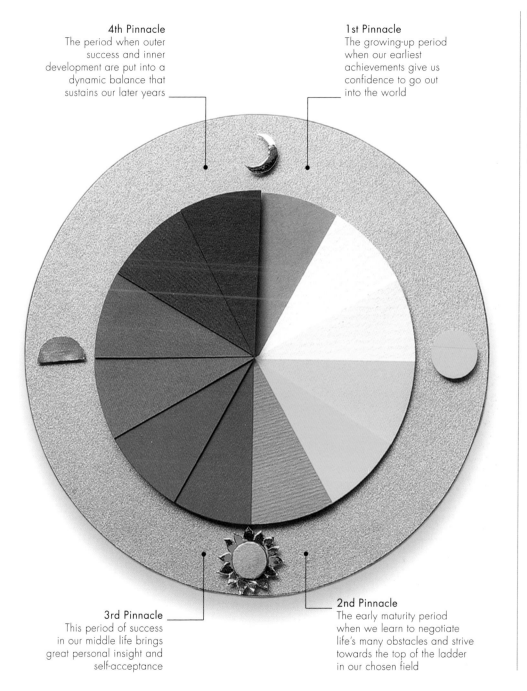

4th Pinnacle
The period when outer success and inner development are put into a dynamic balance that sustains our later years

1st Pinnacle
The growing-up period when our earliest achievements give us confidence to go out into the world

3rd Pinnacle
This period of success in our middle life brings great personal insight and self-acceptance

2nd Pinnacle
The early maturity period when we learn to negotiate life's many obstacles and strive towards the top of the ladder in our chosen field

The Time of Your Life

The Numbers below can apply to any of the four Pinnacle periods – from youth to old age. For example, a teenager will experience a Five Pinnacle Number differently from a 55-year-old. The qualities of the period will be similar but the way in which they are lived out will change. You will also need to take into consideration the Personality Number as it is the medium through which the Pinnacles are expressed.

Pinnacle Numbers Interpreted

1   A period of self-assertion and achievement. This is the time to go for what you want and launch yourself at life. You get out into the world and are recognized for who you really are. You are putting yourself on the map in no uncertain terms. An easier period for outgoing Personality Numbers and not a period for shrinking into the background.

2   A time for relating and learning to live closely and intimately with others. You learn to be a team player and put your individual needs to one side. Co-operation is the theme of this period. This is an easier period for even-numbered Personalities to live through. The vibrations of a Two Pinnacle do not support individual action or ego-assertion.

3   This is the most optimistic period of your life. A time for expanding experiences, knowledge, and social circles. Good for foreign travel or work. You may uncover a talent or gift and work hard to express it. Foreigners may come into your life during this period. New philosophies that challenge your cultural or spiritual background can give you new ways of defining yourself.

4   A period of hard work and little available money. You are learning to structure your time and your talents so that you can reap the rewards later. Life does not feel fun, but ultimately the hard work pays off. Your resources are likely to be stretched due to circumstances beyond your control. For example, it can denote the period in which you establish your domestic situation.

Pinnacle Numbers Interpreted

5

This is a period of many changes. You gain personal freedom by letting go of restricting and limiting patterns and breaking down old structures. You develop your communication and creativity skills. You are out and about and communicating with everyone you meet. It can be the period during which your child leaves home for the first time, for example.

6

Family responsibilities demand your attention during this period. A useful time to learn caring and counselling skills. Good for personal happiness and finances. You may put your money into renovating and beautifying property. An important relationship is often the key event of this period. In fact, all relationships take on greater significance during these years.

7

This is a good period for higher education and taking on research projects. It can also indicate a spiritual search that takes you far from home. A time of deep introspection and self-discovery – you may go into psychotherapy. It could also signify a period of studying alternative healing methods that include a philosophical or mystical module.

8

Getting real is the only description for this period. You have to put your financial life in order. Pension plans, taking out mortgages, and paying loans are the focus. Systems put into place now will be in your life for years after this period is over. This is a good period for flexing your personal power and judging the effect you have on those around you.

9

A period of idealism and awakening to major world issues. The ending of situations that cease to be meaningful for you in the longer term. Development of humanitarian and idealistic values. A good time to find a social group that nourishes your heart. You may need to become a knight in shining armour to protect those less able in your social circle.

Challenges
*Each new step we take in
life can be a challenge.*

CHALLENGE NUMBERS: I The thought of being challenged or
confronting problems can be disconcerting. Yet every day we deal with challenges
without thinking too much about it. Although they sound negative, they do not have
to be experienced that way, as they can offer us freedom from things that hold us
back and keep us locked into the past. We suffer negative effects only if we resist the
demands of challenges. Challenge Numbers run side by side with Pinnacle Numbers.
They illustrate the obstacles and delays that you may encounter in your attempt to
reach the heights of your Pinnacle Numbers. There are nine Challenge Numbers
that result from subtraction. The appearance of the zero is possible when the same
numbers are subtracted from each other. It is suggested by many numerologists that
the appearance of the zero in a name chart indicates an old soul that has come
to Earth to move humanity along its path towards enlightenment.

First day at school
*The way early challenges are handled
can have an effect on how challenges
are dealt with in later life.*

Testing times
Some challenges can be prepared for well in advance.

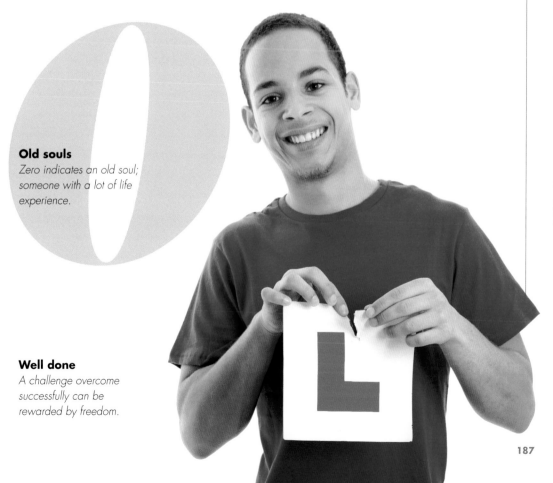

Old souls
Zero indicates an old soul; someone with a lot of life experience.

Well done
A challenge overcome successfully can be rewarded by freedom.

Challenge Numbers: II

Subtraction

Calculating Challenge Numbers is the only time that subtraction is used in numerology.

Challenge Numbers operate in the same time frame as Pinnacle Numbers. To calculate the Challenge Numbers, reverse the process used to calculate the Pinnacle Numbers. We will use a different birth date: 23 August 1969. This gives a Destiny Number 2.

Remember to reduce all double numbers to a single digit before you start to calculate the Challenge Numbers. The subtractions can be made in either direction. This becomes necessary when the first number to be subtracted is greater than the second. In the example below, the birth year (7) is smaller than the birth month (8), but we still arrive at a result of 1.

One strange phenomenon you will notice is that the third and fourth Challenge Numbers are always the same but the Pinnacle number against which the Challenge numbers are working will

Challenge Numbers	
1st Challenge	Birth month minus birth day = 8 – 5 (23) = **3** (Subtract in any order)
2nd Challenge	Birth year minus birth day = 1969 = 7 – 5 = **2**
3rd Challenge	2nd Challenge minus 1st Challenge = 2 – 3 = **1**
4th Challenge	Birth year minus birth month = 7 – 8 = **1**

Remember – the Challenge Numbers run concurrently with the Pinnacle Numbers.

usually differ. Sometimes the result of the subtractions can be a zero. This is the only time it is encountered in numerology. It does not mean that there are no challenges in the person's life. If that were the case, the person would not grow.

In the example below, the two final Challenge Numbers are One. The third Challenge runs alongside a Pinnacle Seven and the final Challenge concurs with a Pinnacle Six. Therefore both One Challenges – of self-assertion and pioneering – emerge out of two very different backgrounds.

Challenge Timing

Timing of Challenges (You will have already calculated these for Pinnacle Numbers).

Age 0–34	Challenge 3
Age 34–43	Challenge 2
Age 43–52	Challenge 1
Age 52 onwards	Challenge 1

CHALLENGE NUMBERS: III

Karma is not out to get you. It brings gifts that attract opportunities for you to clean up your act. You may not like these situations and may turn away from them. If you do, they will continue to let you down. They can be painful to face, but ultimately they teach you about letting go of old attitudes and moving beyond their restrictions. Sometimes you may need to let go of the urge to run away as you have in the past. There is no hard and fast rule about how you deal with challenges. Challenge Numbers accompany Pinnacle Numbers. They indicate challenges that life throws your way to make you expand beyond outworn habits and patterns. Both Pinnacles and Challenges present opportunities, each in their own way, for you to develop your potential. They are like the ebb and flow of the ocean tides. Pinnacles expand and Challenges contract. They are calculated from your birth date, and are, therefore, linked to the unfolding of your Destiny Number and hence, your Karma.

New territory
What will I see?
Who will I meet?

Double Dutch?

Reading a novel in a new language can be exhausting.

The deadline

A work challenge might mean that you must burn the midnight oil to get a project finished.

Challenge Numbers: IV

The Challenge Numbers must always be read in tandem with the Pinnacle Numbers. The test for a numerologist is combining all these different elements to produce a coherent prediction for a client. Remember, a challenge is a circumstance that broadens and expands the horizons.

A client with a strong Personality Four may not like this because she prefers things to stay the same. The task here would be to present the idea to her with the minimum of fuss. On the other hand, a client with a strong Personality Three or Five will relish her challenges and seek out new ones.

Challenge Numbers Interpreted

1
Life makes you stand on your own two feet and "walk your talk", as the Native Americans say. All your dependent behaviour comes under scrutiny. This may be a period where you live or work alone. If you rise to this challenge then you can make your mark and get noticed by the right people.

2
Your challenge is to find a balance between your needs and those of people around you. You are learning to live with others, which can be extremely difficult if you are not clear about your needs. This may coincide with a time of caring for others, such as looking after children or an elderly family member.

3
Your challenge is to learn to speak with circumspection or even keep your mouth shut. You will develop other ways of communicating – through the written word perhaps. You may also have to learn to not be so easy-going or forgiving. Justice needs be realistic; a notion which may challenge your idealism.

4
There can be a distinct lack of material resources during this period. Your challenge is to live within your limits and learn to value yourself for being who you are, not for what you have. If you are starting a family during this time then you will need to tighten your personal budget in order to keep food on the table without resentment.

5

You are challenged to dare to take risks, trusting they will work out. You need to learn to have confidence in the Universe and let go of the tight controls you hold on life. This can be a period of learning to trust your own intuition and of not blaming others when things go wrong.

6

You take responsibility for others but feel tied down by them. Your challenge is to learn to give with a willing heart, but also to learn when it is appropriate to say "no". You may start an arts course at this time but may have little confidence in your abilities. The challenge is to do it anyway and put your fears behind you.

7

You find yourself alone and may not like it. The challenge is to find out what it is about you that puts you in this situation and do something about it. Honesty with yourself is needed here. If you decide to go into therapy you may find that others in your group challenge your attitudes and beliefs. The rewards can be enormous, however.

8

You are being challenged to take responsibility for yourself and pay your own bills, and on time. This is the time to get real about your abilities and charge a proper fee for them. It is the point in life where you can either become a professional or stay an amateur. Your fees will reflect your choice.

9

You are being challenged to stand by your beliefs and be counted. No more hiding behind an easy "front". You may prefer to spend quiet evenings watching television, but your local youth group needs someone to coach the sports team. It could be you, but it requires effort.

0

Your challenge is to align your life with the universal principles that underlie it. Your vision of a better world is attainable, but you must let go of the small concerns that hold you back from this huge responsibility. The zero implies that once you decide to go for it, then support will come from the most unexpected sources.

THE PERSONAL YEAR: 1

The Personal Years symbolize the experiences you have from birthday to birthday, through each nine-year cycle. They begin with a One year and end the process nine years later. They do not offer details about what will happen, but they do offer hints and the meaning of each year. Some numerologists calculate the Personal Year as being from January of each year. You can, if you prefer, start the Personal Year on a person's actual birthday, because only one twelfth of the population is born in January. "Personal" indicates that it is calculated for each person. Therefore, your year should start on the anniversary of your birth.

The Personal Year works for individuals, but it also works for the world. The last hundred years (the twentieth century) add up to One for those in the Western world who use Common Era (CE) reckoning. It was a century for the development of the individual (or individualization) that started with the advent of the psychoanalysis theories of Drs. Freud and Jung. This century (twenty-first) is a Two, which implies that co-operation and relationships are the keywords for the next one hundred years – this gives us all something to look forward to.

Birthdays
Your year should start on the anniversary of your birth.

100

Mark of an era
Each century has its own particular numerological signature.

Age of individualization
The twentieth century was the era of the birth of personal development according to Drs. Freud (below) and Jung. The Suffragette movement (below, far left) won the vote for women in Britain, while the First World War (below, left) was a landmark in modern history. The 1969 Moon landing (below, right) – during a Seven year – was a milestone in human development. It was the most distant boundary crossing yet.

Personal Years One to Five

Happy birthday
A brand new Personal Year.

The Personal Year is very easy to calculate – simply add the day of birth to the month of birth. Add the total to the number of the present year.

Using data from when Jayne had her consultation in 1999: 6th December = 6 + 12 = 18 = 9. Her current year was 1999 = 28 = 1. Add this to the previous total – 9 + 1 = 1. Therefore Jayne was in a One Personal Year. Remember that her year started from her birthday and not from 1 January 1999. Even though her birthday falls at the end of the year, Jayne still experienced her Personal Year calculated from her birthday through to December 1999. For example, when she began her homoeopathy training in 1995, she was in a Personal Year Five, which started on 6 December 1994. This study began in a year symbolized by freedom. It was a period of breaking away from old concepts of health and healing that she had been raised with. Remember that behind every Personal Year is the number of the year itself. For example, 1994 was a Five year and 1999, a One year.

Many numerology texts state that the Personal Year begins for everyone on 1 January, but not everyone is born on that day. A birthday is an important day, bringing new energy and changes into your life. The years that are easiest and seem to pass most quickly are those that resonate with a number within the core numbers of your Personality or Destiny Numbers.

1

This is the year of new beginnings, starting afresh, launching new enterprises, and births of all kinds. Many people start their families during a One year. Projects begun will develop through all the stages of the nine-year cycle. Odd numbers find it easy. Fours and Eights struggle. There is an unconscious response to a One Personal Year that puts a spring in the step, no matter what your age.

2

A year of co-operation, marriage, moving in with a lover, taking on a business partner. It is a year of sharing and taking the needs of others into account. Many people find it an emotional period. Odd numbers feel wrong-footed throughout the year. Even numbers enjoy it. Sharing is the key to a Two Personal Year. Nothing must be shouldered alone – help is at hand from others, you just have to ask for it.

3

This is a period of exploration, experiencing ideas, philosophies, new countries, and creativity. The urge to communicate is strong. This is a good time to finish that novel in the bottom drawer of your desk. Start thinking of yourself again. Even numbers feel their security is threatened.

4

This can be a most difficult year for some people. A good period for putting structure into your life. You may be in a financial hole. You hone your skills, behave like a true professional, reassess your personal appearance, and get out into the marketplace. Fours love it. Threes and Fives feel imprisoned.

5

Some find this a relief after the previous year. Life moves on creatively. This is a good year to take a long trip overseas or launch a new creative venture. A year of having babies, either of the mind or body. Freedom from routine is the keynote. Twos are uncomfortable. Fours resist it.

THE PERSONAL YEAR: II

The decades of the last century are accurately described by the numbers of the Personal Years. Each decade is known by its number – the Twenties, the Forties, the Eighties, for example. The qualities of the number are encapsulated in the ten-year period, although most decades seem to warm to their own particular theme a couple of years after they start. The Twenties was a decade of experimenting with relationships. Jazz music provided the soundtrack and people danced the night away together. The Thirties was a decade of exploration by air. The Forties was a decade of austerity and wars. The Fifties was a decade of rebellion. The teenager was born. The Sixties gave us the "Summer of Love" and new developments in art and music. The Seventies was a decade of overland travel to mystical experiences. The Eighties was the decade in which power dressing and champagne were the order of the day. The Nineties saw the collapse of totalitarian regimes. The 'Aughts' saw the development of global online communication.

The Twenties
After the horrors of the First World War everyone was in love with life.

The Thirties
This was the decade of easier long-distance travel.

The Fifties
This was a time of freedom and youthful exuberance.

The Sixties
This was a time of liberation and free love.

Personal Years
Six to Twenty-two

New year
This is a time to celebrate and make new personal resolutions.

The Personal Years continue the process of development from the beginning, at number One, to the symbolism of Six and on through to number Nine. The Master Number Eleven is rare, but each decade has a Twenty-two year. Eleven Personal Years appeared twice in the last century, these were 1901 and 1910. In the first few years of this century, they will be 2009, 2011, and 2018. This suggests that events could occur that will have an echo of the qualities embodied by Eleven and experienced during those two years in the previous century.

A new Personal Year can be like a breath of fresh air, especially if the old year was not compatible with the Personality Number. For example, a Four Personal Year can feel like a jail sentence to a Personality Five person if they do not already have a structure in place in their lives.

On the other hand, it can also be the year when good work is achieved by focusing on the essentials and putting extraneous concerns to one side. After all, it is only for 12 months and the rewards can be colossal.

A Personality Two will enjoy a Six Personal Year because of positive developments within relationships and in the family circle.

An Eight Personal Year for a Nine Personality can be a good time to apply for funding for the pet projects that Nines always have going.

Personal concerns are lovingly put aside as others need you more. An elderly parent may need help or a grandchild may be born. Property changes such as a new home or building extensions are on the cards. Ones might feel trapped. Fours, Sixes, and Eights throw themselves into the year with glee.

This is a good year for getting your research project under way. Some people enter psychotherapy or analysis to explore their patterns. You are extra-sensitive to music, colour, and movies during this time. You may begin a spiritual search. Eights and Fours are suspicious. Odd numbers are happy.

This is a year of planning, prioritising what is worth pursuing and leaving behind what is not. There will be losses, endings and rebirths. New people you meet during this year will be with you for a purpose, for them as well as for you. All relationships will be intense and may reveal deep-rooted inner patterns.

The end of the process that started Nine years ago. Relationships past their sell-by date, habitual ways of behaving, even old clothes that no longer fit can all go now. You may find a new idealism growing within you that could propel you onto a larger stage than before. Realistic action for change is the keynote. Can be uncomfortable for all numbers unless they are willing to make changes in their lives.

This can be a time of great insight and expansion of consciousness about yourself, the world, and your place in the whole scheme of things. The Master Numbers reduce to Two and Four – good practical numbers with their feet firmly on the ground (much needed during these special Personal Years).

LINKS WITH
ASTROLOGY & TAROT

Many numerologists have a good working knowledge of astrology or Tarot reading. In fact, many numerologists, astrologers, and Tarot readers combine all three disciplines during client consultations. Astrology is linked to numerology in that each of the planets has a numerical value. The Tarot is a combination of two packs of cards – the Major and Minor Arcana. The Major Arcana, believed by many Tarot experts to be the older of the two, assigns numerical values to each picture card. There are 22 cards and they describe the Soul's journey through life. Once you become confident with your numerology calculations, planetary rulerships and corresponding Tarot cards can be incorporated into a consultation to give your client a broader picture.

Numerology & Astrology: I

Planets and numbers
The earliest astrologers analysed the effects of the planets upon human beings.

Each planet has its own number associated with it. These planetary links illustrate early astronomers' insights into the Solar System.

The Sun & Number One

Solar types are ambitious, outgoing, adventurous, competitive, and love starting projects.

The Moon & Number Two

Lunar types are sensitive, impressionable, maternal, and inconstant.

Jupiter & Number Three

Expansive in both mind and body, these types love life and are naturally mystical.

Earth & Number Four

Earthy types take their time, are practical, and loaded with common sense.

Mercury & Number Five

Mercurial types are quick-witted, mentally alert, and studious.

Venus & Number Six

Often physically beautiful, people with this influence seek balance.

Neptune & Number Seven

This poet, mystic, and cosmic cowboy dissolves boundaries and merges with the Divine.

Saturn & Number Eight

Saturn adds boundaries, holds things
in place, and gives them shape.

Mars & Number Nine

Mars types are practical idealists who
assert their wills to get the job done and
defend their beliefs.

Uranus & Number Eleven

Sudden insights make people influenced
by Uranus catalysts for change, volcanic in
nature, humanitarian, and political.

Pluto & Number Twenty-two

Pluto brings deep transformation with Earth-
shaking power and changes things forever.

The Night Sky

The earliest astrological information was
gathered to aid crop planting and animal
husbandry, and to judge the outcomes of
tribal conflicts.

NUMEROLOGY & ASTROLOGY: II

Numbers in astrology are mirrored in numerology, with the exception of the Master Numbers. The most important numbers are Five, Seven, Nine, and Twelve. Seven is the number of the visible planets and is considered lucky by many cultures. Five and Nine are the so-called "good" houses that bring positive lessons from past lives. They are associated with expansion, philosophy, travel, and creativity (regarding both children and works of art). Twelve is the number of the signs of the zodiac and the houses on the astrological birth chart. The twelvefold division is found in many cultures – the twelve tribes of Israel, for example. The numbers Four, Eight, and Twelve, particularly, are considered to be difficult numbers from the outside that challenge the assumptions and security of an individual.

The planets
These celestial bodies are wanderers that orbit the Sun against a background of stars.

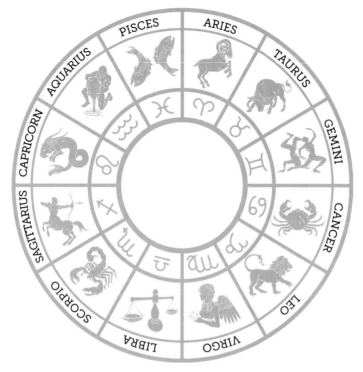

The zodiac
*Greek for "zoo", most of the signs
of the zodiac symbolize animals.*

Destination
*Life is regarded as a journey
in many mystical and
philosophical teachings.*

Numerology & Astrology: III

Ancient symbols
Many cultures have their own zodiac showing animals indigenous to their region.

Astrology is a good system for timing events, but sometimes what is expected does not happen. No matter how the astrologer examines the chart and adjusts the birth time, things just do not work out. Western astrology has its equivalent in numerology with the numbers of the planets, but has no block-timing system like the Pinnacle/ Challenge Numbers. Vedic, or Hindu, astrology operates its own internal block-timing periods however, and frequently uses numerology as an extra tool.

Without understanding how Pinnacle and Challenge Numbers affect a life, a Western astrologer is missing a valuable predictive tool. Vedic, or Hindu, astrology is a very different and much older system. It uses its own particular system for prediction using blocks of time, called *Dasas*, that are similar to Pinnacle Number periods. It has also developed its own system of numerology.

Life cycles

The nine-year periods can act as a backdrop to any seemingly positive event in a person's life. If the Pinnacle Number and the Personal Year Number indicate that someone will experience delays and struggles, no amount of positive good cheer will take away their negative Karmic influences. Many times you may find that the Challenge and Personal Year Numbers gang up together and play havoc with the good influences from a planetary aspect.

Conversely, a positive Pinnacle/ Challenge period can ease the strain of a hard-hitting Saturn visit to a birth chart. It does not mean that its effects go away, but that an individual under this influence will surrender willingly to the Karmic demands that Saturn makes.

What is important about combining numerology with astrology is that you can offer more information to your clients. It enables you to build up a useful picture of how the energies of both systems will interact in your clients' lives. This extra information will help them to make better choices based on more reliable data.

Time Flies

Both astrology and numerology are valid systems for predicting character and trends. Therefore they must both impact on an individual life and must be considered together.

NUMEROLOGY AND THE TAROT

The Tarot is an ancient book in pictorial form that is an esoteric record of human development and spiritual growth. The Tarot pack is made up of two distinctly separate decks. The first is the Major Arcana, which contains 22 cards. The second, the Minor Arcana, is more like a familiar pack of playing cards, and consists of four suits, each of 13 cards, representing the Four Elements. The 22 cards of the Major Arcana have distinct links with both numerology and astrology, just as you would expect. They describe, almost like a strip cartoon, the movement of an individual on a journey towards wholeness – or, in terms of Jungian psychology, going through the process of becoming an individual. Many Tarot readers incorporate the information gleaned from numerology into their readings to provide clients with extra hints regarding the messages encoded in the images.

The Lovers
The Sixth card in the series, this is the card of relationships and passion.

The High Priestess
This card has an air of mystery to it and is feminine and psychic.

Strength

In some packs it is the Eighth card and in others the Eleventh.

Wheel of Fortune

The Tenth card implies new beginnings and has similar qualities to Number One.

The Tarot's Single Numerals

The Book of Life

The Tarot acts like a map for the journey through life's peaks and pitfalls.

The Tarot cards have such power to affect people's minds that for centuries they have developed secretly, much as numerology and astrology have done. Today many people use the cards as a map to guide them to higher consciousness.

One – The Magician

This card represents new beginnings. On the table are the four objects of the Minor Arcana – the Wand, the Cup, the Sword, and the Plate.

Two – The Priestess

This indicates intuition and sensitivity. It is associated with the Egyptian goddess Isis and certainly has an air of mystery about it. Sometimes called the Papess, this card has also been linked with Pope Joan.

Three – The Empress

Representing the harvest of the earth and living the good life, this card shows the Horn of Plenty, ever-filled with abundant luxuries.

Four – The Emperor

A powerful man on his throne, unassailable and solid, this card represents the temporal power of the four Kings of the Minor Arcana.

Five – The Pope

The Wise Counsellor communicates wisdom and sound common sense. He teaches the scriptures and holds the keys of the prevailing religion.

Six – The Lovers

This card of passionate sexual relationships is associated with making a choice, but indicates that any decision is correct.

Seven – The Chariot

This card implies movement and travel, and an ability to use one's will to tame the horses that pull the chariot in which the warrior stands.

Eight – Strength

On this card a woman overcomes a wild lion with her inner strength.

Nine – The Hermit

This card indicates that intuition (symbolized by the lantern) is all that guides the traveller.

The Cards

Where did they come from and how do they predict the future? These questions have been asked for hundreds of years.

THE TAROT'S DOUBLE NUMERALS

The following Tarot cards are double numerals that are higher octaves of the single digit cards One to Nine. They show the journey as it becomes more complex, particularly as we grow older. The steps are not the same as the earlier ones, but they hold similar lessons that we must learn along the way. All the cards of the Major Arcana are spiritual in essence since they were conceived to convey spiritual ideas. It has been suggested that the cards are the real treasure of the Knights Templar, because they valued knowledge more highly than material wealth. It has also been suggested that the cards have their roots in Egyptian religious teachings and are the writings of the greatest mystic of all antiquity, the Egyptian Hermes Trismegistus.

Temperance
This card is sometimes called the Angel of Time.

The Devil
This card associated with fate encourages the letting-go of old patterns.

Justice

This Eleven card symbolizes harmony and balance.

The Tower

Some might say it is time to move house when this card appears.

The Final Eleven Cards

Sunshine

*The Sun is one of the most auspicious
cards to be found in the Tarot deck.*

The numbers of the final eleven cards
indicate the final and most difficult
part of the seeker's journey.

Ten – The Wheel of Fortune

The Wheel symbolizes the eternal
Karmic round, the turning of the seasons,
and new life arising from stagnation.

Eleven – Justice

The balancing of good and evil, desire
for equilibrium and mediation is often
represented by the blindfolded figure.

Twelve – The Hanged Man

This card indicates a turning away
from material desires and adopting
a wait-and-see attitude.

Thirteen – Death

This symbolizes struggle and death
of old habits, not physical death.

Fourteen – Temperance

This indicates new life, gifts from the
gods, and is linked with the Eleusinian
Mysteries of death and rebirth.

Fifteen – The Devil

The devil card indicates that it is
time to move on from the bonds of
the physical appetites of greed, lust,
and anger.

Sixteen – The Lightning-struck Tower

The ego struck by a lightning bolt
indicates sudden changes and a
shifting of consciousness.

Seventeen – The Star

The Star promises that the gods accompany
the seeker at all times, and renewal after
the buffeting of ego-loss.

Eighteen – The Moon

This indicates the unpredictable power
of the unconscious mind and a period
of overcoming deep-seated fears and
prejudices.

Nineteen – The Sun

Moving into the bright light of day,
this shows that the childlike qualities of
innocence and joy are reawakening.

Twenty – Judgement

The seeker awakens and realizes that
there is life after death. It signifies the
awakening into eternal consciousness.

Twenty-one – The World

The journey has been completed
and now the seeker must start again
– forever onward.

THE FOOL: ZERO

The Fool is placed at both the beginning and the end of the sequence of Major Arcana cards. It is the card of Zero and Twenty-two. Both Zero and Twenty-two symbolize the names of God in many cultures. They indicate the power of creation and the completeness of the whole. At the beginning of the pack, the Fool represents the Divine Child within us all. It symbolizes the Soul leaping off the edge of reality into matter to incarnate as a human being. It has the qualities of naivety, foolishness, and childlike innocence. Parsifal the Grail-seeker is linked with the Fool. At the end of the pack, the Fool represents the Soul stepping off the edge of a precipice in readiness for returning home. It is a symbol for a feeling or quality that is imbued with "divine homesickness" and a yearning to be reunited with God.

Blissful ignorance
This state has been yearned for by mystics throughout the ages.

The Soul
*Is he leaping out of Life,
or into it?*

Omega
*In every ending
is the seed of a
new beginning.*

...ocence

o the seeker

The Fool
*Is his "divine homesickness" for
heaven or earth?*

219

GLOSSARY

Archetypes
An original model or design that epitomises its purest expression.

Challenge Number
These are the only numbers in numerology that are calculated by subtraction.

Destiny Number (or **Life Path Number**)
This is calculated by adding up the numbers of your date of birth.

Enneagram
A nine-pointed star used to describe the nine modalities of human behaviour.

Even Number
A number that is divisible by other numbers.

Karma Numbers
These show the underlying, mystical patterns operating in your life.

Many Numbers
Numbers that recur in any name chart or personality group.

Master Numbers
Eleven and Twenty-two are considered to symbolize a special destiny.

Missing Numbers
These are missing in a name chart or personality group.

Odd Number
An odd number can never be divided by two. Nine is the only odd number that is divisible by another number.

Personal Year
The sum of the birth day, birth month, and the current year.

Personality Number
Calculated from the sum of the numbers in a name chart.

Universal Number
The archetype of a particular number that contains all of its positive qualities.

FURTHER READING & WEBSITES

Numerology

Buchanan, Michelle. *Numerology: Discover Your Future, Life Purpose and Destiny from Your Birth Date and Name.* Hay House UK, 2015.

Johari, Harish. *Numerology: With Tantra, Ayurveda, and Astrology.* Destiny Books, 1990.

Ngan, Nicolas David. *Your Soul Contract Decoded: Discovering the Spiritual Map of Your Life with Numerology.* Watkins Publishing Ltd, 2013.

Phillips, David A. *The Complete Book of Numerology: Discovering Your Inner Self.* Hay House UK, 2009.

Rose, Mia. *Numerology: The Ultimate Guide to Uncovering Your Future, Creating Success and Making Your Dreams a Reality Using the Art and Science of Numbers.* CreateSpace Independent Publishing Platform, 2014.

Simpson, Jean. *Numerology (Idiot's Guides).* Alpha Books, 2014.

Tarot

Burger, Evelin and Fiebig, Johannes. *Complete Book of Tarot Spreads.* Sterling, 2014.

Chamberlain, Lisa. *Tarot for Beginners: A Guide to Psychic Tarot Reading, Real Tarot Card Meanings, and Simple Tarot Spreads.* CreateSpace Independent Publishing Platform, 2015.

Louis, Anthony. *Llewellyn's Complete Book of Tarot: A Comprehensive Guide.* Llewellyn, 2016.

Websites

www.spiritlink.com
For everything from Numerology to restaurants.

www.sun-angel.com
Numerology horoscopes.

www.hayhouse.co.uk
Tarot, Numerology and Angel cards.

Astrology and Numerology

www.cafeastrology.com
Free reports and calculations.

www.dawnekovan.com
Learning online.

INDEX

ACKNOWLEDGEMENTS

I would like to thank everyone at Ivy Press, particularly my two editors Caroline Earle and April McCroskie. Thank you also to Robert for the cups of tea and my three boys, Scott, Jared, and Eliot, for the emails that kept me in contact with the outside world as I worked towards my deadlines. The publisher would like to thank Star Brewery Pottery, Lewes; The Boxroom, Lewes; The Pine Chest, Lewes; Kenneth Clark Ceramics, Lewes, for the kind loan of props.

PICTURE ACKNOWLEDGEMENTS

Tarot Cards

The following illustrations are reproduced by permission of HarperCollins Publishers Ltd. UK. The Arthurian Tarot © Caitlin and John Matthews/Miranda Gray: 219t. The William Blake Tarot © Ed Buryn: 219b.

akg-images: 20; 47TR; /Science Source: 47B.

Alamy Stock Photo/ 19th era: 78B; AF archive: 77; Pictorial Press Ltd: 54, 199B; Chronicle: 139; dieKleinert: 114; Masterpics: 87R; Natalia Postolatii: 175TR; shinypix: 123; Splash News: 129; YAY Media AS: 109.

Bridgeman Images: 103T; /From Russia with Love by Terence Young with Sean Connery, 1963: 22B; Palazzo Ducale, Mantua, Lombardy, Italy: 111B; Palazzo Vecchio (Palazzo della Signoria) Florence, Italy: 93, 152; © British Library Board. All Rights Reserved: 91T; Photo © Leicester Arts & Museums: 95b; Terme Museum, Rome, Italy: 107B; Vatican Museums and Galleries, Vatican City: 90T; Prado, Madrid, Spain: 114.

Fletcher Family Archive: 134-135b all.

Getty Images/ DEA/G. DAGLI ORTI: 90B; Colin Anderson: 119B; Sunset Boulevard: 199M; Caiaimage/Martin Barraud: 119T; Edward G. Malindine: 199T; Joseph Scherschel: 83T; mbbirdy: 87L; Bettmann: 55TR; Dan Mullan: 58B; Dave J Hogan: 43TL; Gie Knaeps: 58T; Handout: 39; Jamie McCarthy: 35B; Photo Josse/Leemage: 51T; Roman: 35TL; Ariel Skelley: 102B, 131T; Ben A. Pruchnie: 14B; Buyenlarge: 14T; Heritage Images: 107T; Historical: 110B; Hulton Archive: 15B; Keystone: 16; Kinzie Riehm: 186; Matthew Peyton: 59TL; Max Mumby/Indigo: 59TR; Michael Betts: 138B; Mikael Vaisanen: 96; Phillipp Schmidli: 26B; Radius images: 118B; RDA/RETIRED: 27TR; Richard T. Nowitz: 122L; Robert Daly: 94.

iStock/ julos: 191; 4nadia: 207B; Asia Images: 175BR; CagriOner: 131B; CTRPhotos: 115B; ferrantraite: 165; filipefrazao: 66B; fotostorm: 135; Imgorthand: 82T; isabeltp: 66T; LdF: 35TR; lujing: 79T; monkeybusinessimages: 143R; MorelSO: 67; NicoElNino: 190-191; ozenli: 175L; Spotmatik: 78T; Steve Debenport: 86T; Vesna Andjic: 191; skodonnell: 162B.

NASA: 34T, 38, 42T, 69; 195R; 206.

REX/ GEORGE KONIG: 23TL.

Shutterstock/ Africa Studio: 111T; Aisyaqilumaranas: 79; bigjom jom: 210B, 210BR, 211R, 211L, 214L, 215L, 215R, 218; Binh Thanh Bui: 171BR; catwalker: 15TL; chombosan: 151B; Christos Georghiou: 207T; CP DC Press: 43TR; Dabarti CGI: 51BL; Dean Brobot: 166; Dmitry Pichugin: 167T; Doug Lemke: 61; edella: 39; Ermolaev Alexander: 195T; ESB Professional: 171T; Everett Historical: 15TR; FamVeld: 130T; Featureflash Photo Agency: 76; Filip Fuxa: 51BR; happy photo; hartphotography: 187B; Jacob Lund: 73; Krista Kennell: 62B; LStockStudio: 187T; Luis Louro: 97; Maknach_S: 151T; mark reinstein: 31TL; Mary Frost: 22T; Marzolino: 92; Masson: 160; Maxx-Studio: 167B; Monkey Business Images: 163B, 170; Morphart Creation: 117; nullplus: 163T; Oksana Kuzmina: 102T; Oleksiy Rezin: 82B; paulart: 150B; Pavle Bugarski: 24; Peteri: 47TL; Prostock-studio: 55TL; Randy Mira-montez: 30B; Rawpixel.com: 143L; Repina Valeriya: 62-3, 65; Romariolen: 83B; Ruslan Guzov: 171BL; saraporn: 95T; Silver Spiral Arts: 46; Sova Vitalij: 44; Syda Productions: 130B, 134; TuiPhotoEngineer: 27TL; Vgstockstudio: 86B; Viorel Sima: 110T; volkovslava: 142B, 214R; wavebreakmedia: 103B, 105; KucherAV: 174.

Wikimedia Commons: 39, 50; /Imperial War Museums: 194L; James Willis Sayre: 23TR; Kyle Hoobin: 62T; Library of Congress: 195L; Metropolitan Museum: 49; Project Gutenberg: 30T, 31TR.